Praise f
Finding Our Families

"With wise, compassionate, practical, and innovative advice, Wendy Kramer and Naomi Cahn guide readers through the ever-unfolding world of donor conception and address the complexities—and rewards—that come when people search for donors and other genetic connections. *Finding Our Families* is that rare book you will read and return to again and again over time, appreciating and understanding it in different ways as you explore and discover new forms of kinship."

—ELLEN GLAZER, LICSW, coauthor of *Having Your Baby Through Egg Donation*

"Kramer and Cahn have written a much-needed guide for the offspring of sperm or eggs from usually anonymous providers, as well as for their parents and even the providers themselves. *Finding Our Families* is clear and straightforward and will be immensely useful for the vast and growing numbers of donor-conceived children and their families. The authors, refreshingly, come out strongly against anonymity and in favor of our having the right to know from whom we come."

—BARRY STEVENS, filmmaker and writer
of *Bio-Dad* and the Emmy-nominated *Offspring*

"*Finding Our Families* gently stretches us to consider the experiences of all those involved in helping to make our families. As a psychotherapist, a lesbian, and the mother of a donor-conceived child, I finished this book a more compassionate and forgiving person. There is nothing more powerful than the truth."

—LIZ MARGOLIES, founder and executive
director, National LGBT Cancer Network

"This groundbreaking book affirms what donor-conceived people have been telling us: they want, need, and deserve the truth about their genetic origins and the right to decide for themselves whether to seek contact with their donor and/or half siblings."

—DIANE ALLEN, cofounder and executive director, Infertility Network (Canada)

"The one thing we as human beings deserve more than anything else is our own personal truth. Wendy Kramer and Naomi Cahn have long fought for this right, even before it was fashionable to do so. These well-respected advocates for the donor-conceived and their families bring outspoken tenacity and audacious courage to the pages of this significant book."

—COREY WHELAN, program director, American Fertility Association,
and author of *Combating Infertility During Military Service*

Mar 2018

"*Finding Our Families* isn't just a good and important book—it's a necessary one."

—ADAM PERTMAN, executive director, Evan B. Donaldson
Adoption Institute, and author of *Adoption Nation*

"*Finding Our Families* is a must read for anyone, in any part, of the donor conception process. Comprehensive, thoughtful, and full-hearted, this book addresses the myriad issues that can arise in donor families." —SUSAN FRANKEL, marriage and family therapist

"*Finding Our Families* is an invaluable resource for everyone involved in the field of third-party reproductive medicine. It is informative for professionals and families alike, and condenses complex processes into manageable bites that are understandable and helpful. It is also beautifully written, cohesive in its organization, and captivating in its personal and sensitive style. I could not put it down, and can't wait to order multiple copies for current and former clients who are considering or have conceived through sperm or egg donation. The book is like a concluding paragraph to my passionate efforts to illuminate important, long-term emotional issues hidden within the practice of anonymity and secrecy."

—PATRICIA P. MAHLSTEDT, psychologist

"Clearly written and well organized, this is an indispensable guide for all those who are part of families formed with donated eggs or sperm."

—RENE ALMELING, assistant professor of sociology, Yale University,
and author of *Sex Cells: The Medical Market for Eggs and Sperm*

"Kramer and Cahn have written a heartfelt, practical, easy-to-read, step-by-step book that is indispensable for all members of families with donor-conceived children. *Finding Our Families* includes empathetic and useful sections about meeting the donors, connecting with half siblings and their families, recognizing potential outcomes, and handling rejection of efforts to connect. This book is must reading for all members of the family."

—JENNIFER P. SCHNEIDER, M.D., Ph.D., author of *Understand
Yourself, Understand Your Partner*

"This is a wonderful and much-needed book for donor-conceived kids and their families. I am impressed with the depth of the insights, the references to the latest research in the field, and the depth of detail with regard to conducting searches for donors and half siblings through the Donor Sibling Registry. This kind of information goes a long way toward demystifying that process and will allay the fears of those who want to make contact with their donors and/or half siblings." —KIM KLUGER-BELL, LMFT

"*Finding Our Families* offers guidance in this uncharted territory to people thinking of using a donor, parents who have a donor child, donor-conceived people searching for half siblings or donor parents, and the donors themselves. Useful information for those personally touched by donor reproduction and for those interested in learning more about a field where science outpaces the current social, ethical, and legal constructs."

—KAREN GOTTLIEB, Ph.D., J.D., privacy advocate

"An invaluable resource for all those searching for their donor or donor siblings through the Donor Sibling Registry."

—SUSAN GOLOMBOK, Ph.D., Centre for Family research, University of Cambridge

AVERY

a member of Penguin Group (USA)

New York

Finding
Our
Families

A First-of-Its-Kind Book
for Donor-Conceived People
and Their Families

Wendy Kramer and Naomi Cahn

Published by the Penguin Group
Penguin Group (USA) LLC
375 Hudson Street
New York, New York 10014

USA · Canada · UK · Ireland · Australia
New Zealand · India · South Africa · China

penguin.com
A Penguin Random House Company

Most Avery books are available at special quantity discounts for bulk purchase for sales promotions,
premiums, fund-raising, and educational needs. Special books or book excerpts also can be created
to fit specific needs. For details, write: Special.Markets@us.penguingroup.com.

Library of Congress Cataloging-in-Publication Data

Kramer, Wendy, date.
Finding our families: a first-of-its-kind book for donor-conceived
people and their families / Wendy Kramer, Naomi Cahn.
p.   cm.
ISBN 978-1-58333-526-0
1. Birthparents—United States—Identification.   2. Children of sperm donors—United States.
I. Cahn, Naomi R.   II. Title.
HV875.55.K73   2013   2013025492
362.82'9—dc23

Printed in the United States of America
1   3   5   7   9   10   8   6   4   2

BOOK DESIGN BY EMILY S. HERRICK

For Ryan, his donor family,
and for the many Donor Sibling Registry members
who have shared their lives with me
—W.K.

To my family
and to the visionary efforts
of the Donor Sibling Registry
—N.C.

contents

introduction

There are only two lasting bequests we can hope
to give our children. One is roots; the other wings.

· HODDING CARTER ·

WE LEARN THE BASIC STORY OF WHERE WE CAME
from around the same time we learn to read: "A boy and a girl,
sittin' in a tree, K-I-S-S-I-N-G! First comes love, then comes marriage, then
comes the girl with a baby carriage!" But it turns out that this basic story
isn't exactly universal. Sometimes two boys or two girls fall in love. Sometimes one girl decides to raise the baby she wants without any help from
a boy; and sometimes when it's a boy and a girl in the tree, the expected
baby never materializes, even after rounds of expensive, stressful fertility treatments. Thanks to advances in reproductive technologies, these
versions of the story can still lead to happy families for lots of hopeful
parents. But someday, the baby outgrows the carriage and begins to ask
questions: Where do babies come from? Where did I come from? Do I have
a dad? Why do I have brown eyes when you both have blue eyes?

It's possible that there are well over a million people alive today who
were conceived with donor sperm, tens of thousands who were conceived

with donor eggs, and thousands more who were created with donated embryos, from both a donor egg and donor sperm. Since most donors are still anonymous, this represents an enormous number of children who will grow up with limited information about their family health history and ancestry, and with no information about other people born from the same donor, their half siblings.

This "not knowing" can feel different at different stages of life. A young child may not show much curiosity about her half siblings or her donor, but a teen in the throes of identity formation may feel a need to know about his genetic relatives and their history in order to become his adult self. This is a virtually universal feeling, and it may have extra resonance for those in donor families. Bruce Springsteen summarized these feelings when, as he accepted the Family Heritage Award at Ellis Island, he observed: "You can't really know who you are and where you're going unless you know where you came from."[1]

It has become evident that a lesson learned long ago in the adoption world applies to donor families as well: human beings want to know where they come from. It was long assumed that donor-conceived people need not know the truth of their origins—and that they should simply be glad to exist. For decades, doctors and employees at fertility clinics and sperm banks told parents never to tell anyone that they used donor eggs or sperm so that the parents could hide their infertility and so that their children would never ask questions. Yet the past couple of decades have demonstrated this position's lack of sensitivity, case by case and story by story. Instead of living in blissful ignorance, children sometimes have an unsettling sense of distance from family; if they stumble across the truth, as often happens, they are likely to feel betrayed. On the other hand, children who know the truth and seek out their genetic relatives report having richer lives, more sources of moral support, and stronger relationships with the parents who have raised them.

We believe that knowing about your origins is not only an innate desire but also a *right* for all donor-conceived people. We believe that disclosure is in the best interests of the donor-conceived child, his or her family, and the donor. We believe that a donor-conceived child's interest in searching for her unknown genetic family must be honored.

Children thrive on honesty. Telling donor-conceived children about their conception as early as possible gives them critical information about their origins. And, even if they are uncomfortable saying so explicitly, some children who have not been told the truth may have a subtle, unshakable sense of difference within the family. As more donor families begin to tell their children about their donor conception early on in their child's life, we've heard from them—thousands of people all around the world—testifying to the success of this open and honest method.

If the desire for a biological connection is strong enough to make adults choose donor conception, then it is the ultimate double standard to imagine that the desire for a biological connection will not be felt just as strongly by the donor-conceived child that is born. This natural curiosity should be supported by parents, by the fertility industry, and by the rest of us.

"People who know both of their biological parents find it hard to grasp the enormity of what I am missing. Simply having information about the sort of people your parents are, and what things they are capable of doing, creates a baseline that you don't realize is comforting unless you have to live without it."

—*Ted, donor-conceived adult*

The Donor Sibling Registry (DSR), the largest Web site where members of the donor community can find each other and share their experiences, has revealed the true magnitude of this natural genetic longing. Before the DSR, there was no easy or effective way for donors and families to connect with each other. For more than a dozen years, the DSR has been their hub. Every day there are connections made on the site. Every month more than ten thousand people visit, looking for information, advice, support, and family.

As cofounder and director of the Donor Sibling Registry, author Wendy Kramer has listened to their stories, and she has been at the forefront of research around the world into the experiences of donor-conceived people, parents, and donors. She shares what she has learned from connecting with these thousands of people and from raising her own donor-conceived son in this very first collection of advice for donor families. Author Naomi Cahn is a law professor who writes and teaches at the vanguard of family law and reproductive technology. Together, we've designed this compendium of advice for donor families to foster happy and healthy relationships in your immediate families and also within your new donor families.

In the chapters that follow, we will guide would-be parents considering having children through donor eggs and sperm; donor-conceived offspring bravely trying to puzzle out their origins; parents wondering how to tell their children that they were donor-conceived and also how best to support their children's desire to connect with their genetic relatives; and adults who want to connect with one another because they have used the same donor, who want to share information and form new communities, or who want to know what to do when they discover 150 half siblings.

"I was donor-conceived fifteen years ago, and to this day, due in part to my mother's successful parenting, I have never once felt anger or hurt of any sort for being donor-conceived. Indeed, I am curious about my roots, but I am who I am, and knowing my father wouldn't change that. The truth is, not knowing my father is not something I think about on a day-to-day basis. It's not that I ignore it, but having known my birth story since I was only two years old has made it a part of my life that I embrace and accept."

—*Ryan Kramer, Wendy's son (2005)*

Wendy conceived Ryan with donor sperm in 1989. In September 2000, when Ryan was ten years old, the two of them had just come across some surprising information: when Wendy called the sperm bank for more information about their donor, an inexperienced sperm bank employee accidentally revealed that there were several other children born from the same donor that Wendy used, Donor 1058. As soon as Ryan found out, all he wanted to know was, "When can I meet them?" Wendy and Ryan wondered together if he might have any half siblings who also wished to meet him, and even whether his donor might be open to establishing communication. But, as they soon found out, there was no way for them to know if anyone in Ryan's donor family was also curious about him.

The sperm bank would not facilitate mutual-consent contact, even between half siblings who had clearly not signed *any* agreements pertaining to anonymity. There were no search engines or databases to consult. They were at a seemingly dead end.

One morning on the way to school, as Wendy navigated the familiar route through the evergreens of Nederland, Colorado, Ryan told Wendy about something new on the Internet: Yahoo! Groups. They looked at each other and said, "Why not create a Yahoo! Group for donor offspring who would like to meet their half siblings?" They talked about how amazing it would be for Ryan and other donor children to be able to connect with members of their donor family.

Uncertain about whether it would work, they established the Yahoo! Group and posted the first message. That first message explained that they were looking for Ryan's biological relatives and that they were also hoping to create a place for others to search and be found. That was the beginning of the Donor Sibling Registry. For a few months, absolutely nothing happened. Their single post sat lonely on the site. Then they received a few postings from others who were enthusiastic about the site and were hoping to connect too, although none of them were related to Donor 1058.

Over the first few years, the group grew slowly. Then, a feature about the DSR on *Good Morning America* in late 2002 and a 2003 *Oprah* show devoted to the donor insemination industry took membership into the thousands. Because so many matches were being made, Wendy and Ryan decided to take the next step: in late 2003, they built their own Web site to help people find each other. Over the next decade, media exposure— including another *Oprah, 60 Minutes, The Today Show*, and articles in newspapers around the world, including several in the *New York Times*— brought more and more members in search of siblings and donors, and the DSR facilitated thousands of matches.

In 2007, Wendy and Ryan's posting had been on the DSR for almost seven years, although no connection had been made. On a cold February afternoon, they checked the site together, as they did almost every day— but this time, they finally found the message they had been waiting for. It was from another child conceived with the sperm of Donor 1058. Wendy and Ryan sat side by side and read through the posting carefully, trying to control their hopes and fears. They had already suffered some disappointment with potential matches: in one case, the parents did not want to disclose to the children that they were donor-conceived, so there was no one for Ryan to meet; in another case, parents of a half sibling denied the connection. Wendy and Ryan were cautiously optimistic.

This time, the post was from a thirteen-year-old girl who had just signed on to the site with her dad and was astonished to learn that her half brother was the boy whose picture was featured on the DSR's home page—the boy who had actually started it. Finally, Ryan had made a successful match on the DSR. He was the 2,910th person to do so.

Ryan, then sixteen, and Wendy composed a note to Ryan's new half sister and her parents, including their phone number, and submitted it through the DSR. Just a few hours later, the phone rang. It was the half sister's parents. In that first phone conversation, her parents and Wendy agreed that even though they had never met, they didn't feel like strangers—they shared something precious and rare, a genetic connection between their children. Remarkably, Ryan and his half sister have the same birthday. As Wendy had lit three candles on a Superman birthday cake for Ryan, his half sister had been drawing her first breaths, two thousand miles away.

Barely six weeks after that first message, Wendy and Ryan flew to New York to meet his new half sister and her family in Central Park. They spent the first hour asking each other questions, taking pictures, wiping away tears, and hugging. Despite the seventy-five-degree weather, Ryan's half sister put on the University of Colorado sweatshirt Ryan had brought her. It was obvious that each only child was deliriously happy to have found a half sibling. The parents studied the children, looking for—and finding—resemblances. Both half siblings had the same smile and chin. Their profiles were strikingly similar. While their parents had been carefully using the terms "half brother" and "half sister" to describe the relationship, the two of them rejected that description. They insisted, "No. We're just brother and sister."

. . .

Relationships within the world of donor conception are not always established with such sureness and grace. Donor-conceived children are not always as well adjusted as Ryan and his half sister. Some are angry that they grew up not knowing the truth about their origins, and some struggle with the fact that they don't have access to one half of their genetic and cultural history. In most donor-conceived families, the parents don't know the identity of the donor, and the donors have no idea what has happened to their eggs or sperm. The parents may know the donor's hair color, height, college, and profession; they may even have heard the donor's voice collected on an audiotape interview as part of the donor's profile. But they don't know his name or contact information. Until recently, donor-conceived offspring typically weren't even told that one of their biological parents was a donor.

Traditionally, donor eggs and donor sperm have been swaddled in secrecy. When people like Wendy and her husband went to a fertility clinic in 1989, no one said anything to them about the importance of disclosure and a child's right to know the truth. Infertile couples who received donor sperm or eggs rarely ever told their friends or family members, much less their children. Even today, glossy magazines celebrate famous women who have babies at the age of forty-five or even fifty, but they rarely mention that this is almost physically impossible without donor eggs.

In the past decade, the oppressive secrecy surrounding donor conception has started to change, at least within donor-conceived families. There are no national laws that either require or prohibit this information exchange;

the change is coming from within the donor community itself. As a new commitment to openness and honesty emerges, and as parents become increasingly likely to tell their children that they are donor-conceived, many donor offspring are growing up with more information about their origins. A critical mass of donor-conceived children has now reached adulthood, and they are able and eager to articulate their views. People throughout the donor-conceived community are opening up and talking about their experiences. They remind us that the end result of the overwhelming urge to have a baby is not *just* a baby; it's a human being, whose healthy development involves various phases of self-definition and endless questions. This book is full of ways to get answers, and it guides parents and donor-conceived people through the process of telling, reaching out to, and connecting with family.

Some of you may be potential parents, trying to decide whether or not to use an open or willing-to-be-known donor, and wondering just what it will be like to have a child born through donor conception. Or you might already have a donor-conceived child. You may have donated your eggs or sperm. For some of you, there is also a good chance that your parents used donated eggs or sperm to conceive you. If you're among the million or so people who were conceived in this way, you are certainly not alone. Not only do you have a lot in common with many other donor-conceived people, you actually might be related to some of them!

Familiarity with your basic genetic heritage—something as simple as knowing the way your mother's eyes crinkle when she smiles or how your father has struggled with depression—is a steadying influence, one that most people take for granted. But as adoptees have long known, when one parent is a question mark, the search for answers may end up consuming the rest of your life. The blank spaces in your story may fill up with pain. To prevent as much of that pain as possible, we want this book to serve as a strong voice in the movement to discourage secrecy and promote disclosure concerning donor conception, and to foster new ways of defining and expanding family for all of us. As you read and think through and live these issues, be open. Be honest with yourself and your loved ones. It won't always be easy, but you will be rewarded with a clear conscience, a strong family, and the tools you need to explore your donor community.

Openness is the core truth that anchors *Finding Our Families*. This core truth plays out in all three parts of this book: in the introductory chapters on how parents and children can talk about donor conception, in the middle chapters on searching for your donor and half siblings, and in the final chapters, on creating and maintaining your donor community. Although much of our advice is straightforward and simple to follow, it won't always be easy, and we want to give you the tools and support you need for your own exploration of your donor community.

chapter one

The D Word

In every conceivable manner, the family is link to
our past, bridge to our future.

· ALEX HALEY ·

I nvolvement with donor conception is a lifelong process of exploring the meaning of family and connection. Understanding the hidden history of donor conception, getting to know the donor community, and acknowledging the many different connections created by donor conception will help you navigate through your own personal journey. Donor conception challenges the centuries-old image of parenthood based on both marriage and biological connections.

When Wendy and her former husband learned that they could not conceive on their own and decided to use donor sperm, their main focus was on finally being able to have a baby. They knew almost nothing else about the choice they were making: What would it mean to them and to their relationship? To their child? Should they ever even tell their child? These questions did not occur to them, and, at the time, no one even suggested that they should.

Ryan was a year old when Wendy and her husband divorced and parted ways. After noticing dads in other households, two-year-old Ryan asked his mother, "Did my dad die or what?" Wendy was entirely unprepared for this question. Nor was she ready a few years later to have a six-year-old who was adamant about meeting his biological father. And certainly, no one had ever told her about the complexities of connecting with half siblings and the donor. Ever since she first found out she was pregnant with Ryan, Wendy has had to learn from experience what it means to raise a donor-conceived child.

How Did We Get Here?

In 1884, in one of the first reported cases of donor conception, Dr. William Pancoast, a professor at Jefferson Medical College in Philadelphia, anesthetized a woman and then used sperm from the "best-looking" medical student in his class to inseminate her. Although the woman's husband consented, she never knew what had happened and believed that her husband was the biological father of their child. Initiating a long-standing culture of secrecy, the case wasn't even reported in a medical journal until a quarter-century later.

Throughout most of the twentieth century, secrecy was so pervasive that patients were sent home after an insemination, strongly advised to forget anything had ever happened, and warned never to tell anyone about their use of donor sperm. Some were even told to conceal their use of donor sperm from their obstetricians and pediatricians. For married couples, the primary patients, this meant that no one ever had to know that the husband was actually infertile. Doctors might even try to find a donor who looked like the husband, but the recipient woman had to put complete trust in her physician to choose the right donor (even when it ended up being the physician's own sperm that was used). Choosing donor sperm was so contrary to how society thought a family should be built that some courts judged married women who had used donor sperm to be adulterers and decided that their children were illegitimate, even if the husband had consented.

When the first for-profit sperm bank started up in the early 1970s, it was not open to the public: physicians only. By the late 1980s, when more than four hundred sperm bank facilities were in operation, doctors were still their primary customers. In fact, in 1987, 60 percent of federally surveyed sperm bank facilities would sell *only* to doctors, and none would sell only to recipients. If you were trying and failing to get pregnant, your doctor might explain donor conception to you. If you were interested, he or she would procure the sperm without telling you much, if anything, about the donor. You were just supposed to be happy to get your baby. It was better than being inseminated with a stranger's sperm without your knowledge, but hardly a model of transparency.

Sperm banking became increasingly consumer-oriented throughout the 1970s and into the 1980s, as the banks began advertising, and began providing more information, including physical descriptions, of their sperm donors. This gave consumers, rather than doctors, the power to choose the sperm. Other banks began offering consumers the same options, and the AIDS epidemic added incentives for additional safety tests.

Egg provision has a far shorter history: the first documented egg donation occurred in 1984, and scientific breakthroughs since then on egg freezing have facilitated the process. Today, more than fifteen thousand eggs are donated each year, although, of course, not every egg results in a child. In the beginning, egg donors were identified; they were often recipients' relatives or friends. Today, identified donors constitute a very small part of the donation pool and recipients are more likely to use egg-selling agencies, which almost always require their donors to remain anonymous. Egg donation is on the rise, reflecting the promise of technological advancement and the reality that many women want to become mothers after it is too late to use their own eggs. (It is too early to know whether the trend of women freezing their own eggs to preserve fertility will have an effect on the use of donor eggs.)

The Donor Community: Who Are We?

Millions of people, beyond the offspring themselves, are affected by donor conception. Maybe you're a woman who decided that instead of waiting for Mr. Right, you would have a child with Mr. Good Sperm. Perhaps you've found your dream partner, but since you're the same sex, donor conception is your only hope for having a baby. You could be a college student trying to decide whether or not to donate your sperm. Or maybe you and your partner, like one in eight couples in the United States, struggle with infertility. Perhaps you're the grandparent or another family member of a beloved donor-conceived child. As far as we're concerned, all of you, and your offspring, are part of the donor community.

For many decades, infertile heterosexual couples were the primary users of donor sperm, but in recent years there has been a huge demographic shift. Advances in reproductive technology have made heterosexual couples less likely to need donor insemination, and families are increasingly being formed outside of the married heterosexual model. In fact, single women (Single Mothers by Choice or SMCs), both gay and straight, who choose to become parents without partners, as well as lesbian couples, are now the largest groups of donor-sperm users. Women in the United States have been waiting longer to start having children. While the average age of a first-time mother was about twenty-one in 1970, today the average age is approximately twenty-five and the average age of marriage is even later. The pregnancy rates for women who are forty and older have been steadily increasing. And for gay men, finding an egg is critical. The Donor Sibling Registry recently polled its members and found that their profile had shifted along the same lines as the customer base of several sperm banks: approximately 50 percent are single mothers, 33 percent are LGBTQ (Lesbian, Gay, Bisexual, Transgender), and 17 percent are heterosexual couples.

The nonmarital birth rate in the United States is over 40 percent, and while the number of births to teens is falling, the number of births to single women over the age of thirty is increasing. Most of these women do not use donor sperm, but that's changing. There are thousands of women on the DSR who have made the decision to become an SMC after a lot of careful thought. Overwhelmingly they say yes, indeed, parenting is often difficult, and they do sometimes wish they had a partner with whom to share responsibilities, as well as dreams and joy. But they also speak of having discovered inner strength and resources that they never believed they had. Much can be borne for the sake of a baby's smile. They also tell us that they lean on their newfound donor families and the greater donor community.

Seriously Planned Parenthood

For many people, genetic connection is what defines a family. That's what they grow up seeing and being told. Laws assume that blood relatives (or those in legally recognized relationships) will be the ones to make decisions for us when we are ill and to inherit our money when we die. But as the experiences of both adoptive families and of donor-conceived families show, genetics aren't everything, even when it comes to having a baby and caring for a child. Just as a genetic bond alone won't make you a good parent, the lack of one cannot disqualify you.

In fact, studies show that families created by egg and sperm donation often have more positive parent-child relationships than do families created by natural conception, and that parents who used donors tend to have higher levels of emotional involvement with their children. According to a 2004 study, children formed through donor eggs or sperm may give their mothers more than the average amount of joy and inspire greater than average protectiveness; the authors speculated that "women who are unable to have children, because of either their own or their partner's infertility, view their child as precious and are committed and loving parents."[1] The bonds of love in donor families are the same as in any other family, so take comfort knowing that the process may be different, but the result is often the same.

The choice to use donor conception requires lots of soul-searching and legwork.

Here are some questions you may have already considered and, if you haven't yet figured them out, thinking about them now is crucial. Take the time to talk about each one of these issues with your partner and your family:

1. Does it matter *how* you became a parent? Why?
2. What does it mean for you not to know about half of your child's genetic heritage? What does it mean for your child not to know?
3. If you made your decisions with a partner, then did you both feel the same way about becoming a parent and about genetic connections? Do you feel the same way now as when you first made the decision?
4. What do you know about the needs and issues of donor-conceived children?
5. How do your family, friends, and community feel about your decision to use donor conception?

Ideally, people who choose donor conception are prepared for the complicated joys ahead of them before they even start browsing donor profiles. But often they're not. Sperm banks and egg agencies are primarily in the business of making money, not educating donors and parents or helping them sort through existential concerns, so you need to look elsewhere to prepare yourself.

A Few Notes about Terminology

"He is not my 'donor,' he is my father, he was my parents' 'donor.' Terminology is important," Katie emphatically corrected us. Her mother said, "Those of us who have donor children don't call ourselves 'donor families.' We are just a family, like yours. We don't live in a 'donor world,' we live in your world. That would be identifying your family, your existence and world by the method of your or your child's conception. We form 'donor families' when we connect with others; they are members of our 'donor family.' We're all people connected by a single gamete donor."

Chuck, whose parents used donor sperm, explains: "The one term I have a great deal of trouble with is 'donor.' This man did not 'donate' anything, he sold his sperm. 'Donation' means giving something to someone for a good cause or the act of giving to a charity. I do not have a donor. I have a biological father."

The language we use to describe our relationships reveals how we think about ourselves. Over the years, we have learned that terms vary greatly among different types of families, donor offspring, donors, and parents. In this book, we've tried to use a variety of terms, even as we realize that some of them will make some people uncomfortable.

There are no agreed-upon stock terms to describe the person who "donated" sperm or eggs (the donor, the vendor, the genetic father or mother, donor dad or mom, or biological father or mother). In the United States, donors are never really "donors" because they are paid for their sperm or eggs. Parents who are not biologically related to their children might not like the term "nonbio parent," but the term can be useful when trying to differentiate between parents and their experiences.

We don't yet have standard language for the person conceived via donor sperm or eggs (the offspring, donor baby, donor child, or donor-conceived person). It can be challenging for us to even describe our own families, not because language is imprecise but because of the varied emotions associated with the terms. Are we families who have used donor gametes, or are we "donor families"? Are "donor families" only the new people you connect with who share the same donor? Do all families who have used donor conception live in a "donor world"? We know that there are no terms that will make everyone happy.

In fact, various terms that offspring use can be uncomfortable for parents (an issue we explore later in the book). Many offspring insist that the person who donated sperm is not the "donor" but their "biological father." We should respectfully allow donor offspring to choose the labels that are right for them, whether they feel right to parents or not. Don't be afraid of this. Defer to your child's choice; you will learn much about their thoughts on being donor-conceived. As children go through different developmental stages, they may try out different terms when they refer to the donor. Be prepared for your child to try out terms that might not be comfortable for you.

In one study, 751 offspring were asked to select all of the different terms with which they referred to their donors; in response, 42 percent said "donor," 30 percent said "sperm donor," 28 percent said "biological father," 11.5 percent said "donor dad," 8.5 percent used the term "father," and 4.5 percent used the term "genetic father." In other words, whatever terms they used, more than half used the words "father" or "dad" when referring to the donor. By contrast, another study of seventeen hundred *parents* who had used donor sperm chose the language they used to refer to the donors; only 22 percent selected terms that included "father" or "dad." Almost two-thirds used terms that included the word "donor."[2] Word choice profoundly reflects people's differing relationships and perspectives about the person who provided their gametes.

Mark, the father of a young child conceived with a donor egg, explains the choices made in his family: "We bought eggs from a college student, Emma, and she was open to staying in touch with us. We've asked our toddler to call her 'Aunt Emma.'" As Mark's son matures, he may decide to use a more accurate term to refer to the woman who donated eggs to his parents. For young children, simple terms are best. Parents must be careful not to use jargon or euphemisms that minimize the importance of the donor. To parents, the donor might be just a piece of "genetic material" or just a "donated cell," but to a child, the "donor" is half of his genetic identity.

Because fewer families have been formed through egg donation, and even fewer through embryo donation, most of our experience is with families formed through sperm donation, and many of the stories throughout the book involve donor sperm. All of the discussions, however, apply to any family that has used donor gametes. In all of these families, it is important to be *open to new terms and language that change as your life changes.*

chapter two

No Secrets: Telling Is Important!

Honesty is the first chapter
in the book of wisdom.

· THOMAS JEFFERSON ·

Before we become parents, whether we're reflecting on our own upbringing or watching someone lose her temper with a wailing toddler, we all think: "I'm not going to make those same mistakes!" What seems straightforward in theory becomes ambiguous and challenging in emotion-choked, exhausted practice. For those who become parents thanks to donors, the issues are larger than whether the occasional candy bribe is okay, or whether they should conveniently forget the less than wholesome moments from their adolescence. They must find the peace of mind, strength, and imagination to tell their children a creation story that probably doesn't resemble their friends'.

Maybe you knew as soon as you decided to use donor eggs or sperm that you would eventually need to share that information with your someday child. Or maybe you feel somewhat uncomfortable with your use of donor eggs or sperm; maybe you want to protect your child from feelings of difference; or maybe you believe that the means of conception are irrelevant to the life of your family. Maybe you have not yet decided whether to tell. In fact, a majority of married straight couples still don't tell their children if they used donor eggs or sperm to get pregnant.

But reminders about donor conception will come up, perhaps as you try to figure out why your child is so tall, or so good at math, or so outgoing. You might think about it when people on the street ask where your child got his blond hair, when the pediatrician asks for your child's health history, or even when you and your partner hug your child. You may feel overwhelmed by these simple reminders of your child's origins, even if your child has no idea that she is donor-conceived. Or you may feel uncomfortable when friends talk easily about how much their children look like them, or when they share with you their struggles on how to explain to their children that Daddy planted a seed in Mommy. Of course, if you are a same-sex couple, you don't have the same ability to "pass," but you still can face strangers asking you, "So, who was *your* donor?" You must decide how, when, and precisely what to tell your child. This is a challenge, but also an opportunity for you to take a cue from that ideal parent of your pre-kid imagination.

Take comfort in the fact that the story of the birds and the bees is a little different for each family; all parents must make an effort to devise a script that they can comfortably use. The script you develop for your family is critical in setting the stage for how your child will react to this story of origin. You will also call on your script when you talk about donor conception with your family, friends, and community.

What parents are often surprised to realize is that they usually need to work through their own feelings before they can talk to their children. If you don't face your own hesitations and worries, you'll surely risk passing them along to your children. For example, if you feel embarrassed about using donor conception, your child might pick up on that and feel that you are somehow ashamed not only of the method of his conception but also of who he is.

New research supports the truth that Wendy, Ryan, their known donor family, and many others in the DSR community have lived for years: telling your children that they are donor-conceived is good for them and good for you. We debunk the myths that lead people to believe that secrecy is better or to fear that the truth will alienate their children. Obviously, there are risks when it comes to telling. You may have a child who feels uncomfortable with her origins or one who is unable to satisfy her curiosity about her origins or even one who turns away from you. These issues are difficult—for you and for your child. But the benefits of being honest and open with your children far outweigh the risks of not being able to get enough information or answer all of your child's questions. By the time you finish this chapter, we hope you will feel confident about the importance and value of disclosure. You'll realize that it is in your child's best interest to tell her that she is donor-conceived. You will discover that it's right, good, and necessary to be open about your child's conception, sooner rather than later, with your child, with your family, and even with your community.

You may recognize yourself or some of the issues you've faced in the stories below:

Sally was thirty-eight and single, and she felt that time was running out. She really wanted a child. Her job as an advertising executive was secure, but her most recent relationship had been rocky for a few years and had ended after she and her boyfriend decided that they did not want to spend the rest of their lives together. She considered freezing her eggs so they'd be available when she met the right person, but egg freezing can cost upward of $10,000, a frozen egg might never develop into an embryo, and there was no guarantee that she'd ever meet that perfect person. So she decided to have a baby on her own, using donor sperm. She chose the "perfect donor" after looking through numerous profiles from different sperm banks: a premed student who was willing to be contacted by her child when her child turned eighteen.

When Sally became pregnant with Alex, she was thrilled. He is now a happy three-year-old with dimples and light brown hair enjoying his preschool days. Alex has never asked why he has one parent, so Sally has not yet brought up his donor conception. As she puzzles through what to say to him, she has begun looking at some books written especially for young children and is also browsing Web sites for more advice. She suspects that this topic will come up soon, particularly as he meets more children his age, so she knows she'll have to be ready to say something. And she's getting there, preparing herself to talk as openly as she can about his origins. But Sally worries that if she tells her son everything she knows about the donor now, he might feel a great sense of loss at not having this man in their lives. And what if Alex then expresses interest in finding the donor before he turns eighteen? The Daddy Question might, she worries, become more important than the Mommy Presence.

Sally's friends, Nancy and Jasper, tried to have a baby for three years. On Nancy's forty-third birthday, after they had undergone numerous different infertility treatments, their doctor told them that they would need to use donor eggs to get pregnant. At first Nancy was resistant. She wanted her *own* child, a perfect combination of herself and Jasper. She was worried about bonding with a baby who was not genetically related to her. But she overcame her concerns, and Nancy and Jasper found their ideal donor: a college student who looked a little like Nancy and never wanted any information about what happened to her eggs.

After the birth, Nancy's doubts about her relationship with her child evaporated; in her words, "I carried and delivered this baby. I *am* her mother!" Jasper, too, had initially been apprehensive about the use of donor eggs. Since his sperm would be used to fertilize the eggs, what if he felt closer to the child than Nancy did? Their daughter, Julia, is now two years old. Although Sally knows that Nancy and Jasper used donor eggs, very few other friends or family members have *any* idea that Julia and Nancy are not biologically mother and daughter. Nancy and Jasper think that's great; they don't ever want to revisit the pain of not being able to have a child, and they are considering not ever telling Julia anything.

Cathy and Ellen had both grown up envisioning themselves as mothers. Once they were married, they decided that they would take turns becoming pregnant, using the same donor. It was Ellen's turn first. During Ellen's pregnancy, and then after the birth of their son Ben, Cathy was surprised by her feelings. Of course she loved Ben, but she also felt a combination of jealousy, loss, and grief because she was not the one who had carried him. Ellen wanted to tell Ben at an early age everything she knew about his donor, but Cathy was reluctant. She worried that she would feel distanced from Ben and that he might, in turn, reject her. Along the same lines, she did not ever want to be supplanted by the donor. Because she found it difficult to talk about her hesitations, Cathy found it difficult to discuss her feelings with Ellen, so she kept putting off any further conversations about the issue.

Secrecy or Deception?

Secrecy means withholding information that is not owed to the person from which it is kept. Deception is withholding information that is owed. And lying is knowingly giving information that is false.[1]

Secrecy and deception have been intimately intertwined with donor conception. Once upon a time, nondisclosure was standard. Almost no one talked about whether they had used a donor, and they certainly never told their children. Parents didn't need to think about telling because no one ever told them that this might be the right thing to do for their children; because children didn't know they were donor-conceived, they never asked questions. Sperm banks and, more recently, egg donation programs drew on traditional adoption practices by encouraging parents to keep "the secret" in order to protect their "privacy," so that no one would ask potentially uncomfortable questions and so that the family would just blend in. Keeping the secret was seen as protecting the parents from disapproval and the entire family from stress, pain, and embarrassment.

However, that very same stress, pain, and embarrassment that parents were *trying* to avoid often manifested itself in their children. While parents wanted to believe that they were shielding their children from the trauma of learning that they were not biologically related to one of their parents, in fact they were unwittingly passing along this secrecy-induced shame to their children. Even when children didn't know they were donor-conceived, they felt that something was "off" within their family or felt a disconnect with one or both of their parents.

The advice from the fertility industry was powerful, and many people born through donor eggs or sperm still have no idea about their origins. In DSR consult sessions, parents whisper that Wendy is the only one they have ever told about their child's origins and that they do not intend to tell anyone else. They live in fear that their secret will come out, destroying their relationship with their child. They know they are members of the donor community and they want advice and support—but anonymously, so no one else will ever know.

When trying to understand why some heterosexual parents choose to keep "the secret," we have to look a little deeper to uncover the historical stigma associated with not being able to have children the traditional way: shame about being infertile, shame about not being the "real" parent, shame about not being man enough, woman enough, or whole enough. It helps to remember that the historical definition of "family" has been based on the idea of a married husband and wife and their biologically related children, and the possibilities offered by donor conception differ from that image. Even as donor conception expands the meaning of family, we may still not be creating the family we always believed we would have. Consequently, talking about how we formed our family can be difficult.

In all families, there can be tensions over disclosure. Some long to tell but have partners who are adamantly opposed. The parent who has no biological connection may worry about creating an emotional gap in their relationship with their child. Avoiding discomfort might appear to be the easier way to proceed.

But lies hurt. If we hide something, then we are tacitly declaring that the truth shames us and perhaps even that we cannot live with it being known. We are giving it unwarranted power in our interior lives, whether as a nagging worry or a consuming dread. This unnecessary sense of failure and shame can immobilize us and undermine our very ability to parent.

When University of Texas professor Anita Vangelisti asked people about family secrets, she identified three different categories: (a) secrets that you yourself keep from other family members (perhaps you never told your partner everything about your sexual past); (b) secrets that some members of the family keep from others (perhaps you'll never tell your parents how much your partner hates them); and (c) secrets your family keeps from nonfamily members (perhaps you never discuss your infertility in public).[2] Not disclosing donor conception crosses all three categories: you might not tell your child; even if your child knows, you might keep the truth from other family members; or you might keep the truth from anyone outside the family. All of these levels of secrecy can be destructive to you and your family.

In fact, researchers have found that the deeper the family secret, the more likely it is to be perceived as a physical burden, and the researchers have speculated that this could have health effects.[3] This secrecy is a heavy load to carry, and the layers of deception build up. Families in which secrets are kept are less happy than other families. The best-kept secret can warp family life, filling children with anxiety they don't understand, and parents with guilt. Families secure enough to disclose may simply be healthier overall; the kind of open and honest parent-child relationship that allows a family to tell the truth about donor conception all along is probably also the kind of relationship that encourages healthy development in general. This ounce of prevention actually requires high standards and hard work, but it's less painful than the otherwise inevitable pound of cure.

You need to face your fears so your family can move forward. Parents should cultivate pride, recognizing and declaring that their act of conception was one of unconditional love and determination. Anyone who chooses donor conception has already chosen an unconventional path and therefore is, one hopes, strong enough to face its unconventional rewards and challenges. Secrets have a corrupting influence on family life and make us go against our instinct to create open and truthful lines of communication with our children. There are, of course, things in the world we must shield children from, but the depth of our desire to conceive, and the method that we used to conceive, are not among them.

CHECKLIST: UNDERSTANDING YOUR CHILD'S NEEDS

Take a break from your own anxiety to think about how knowing the truth might affect your child today, tomorrow, and far in the future. Consider these questions carefully.

1. To whom does this information belong?

2. Why might your child want to know the truth about his origins? How might this be important to him?

3. Why might your child want to know about his medical and genetic background? Could this help with preventive care?

4. Why might your child want to know about his ancestry and to whom he might be related?

5. Why might your children be curious about their donor families (half siblings and/or their donors)? What will it mean to them to have you support curiosity rather than feel threatened by it? Why might your children want to find them?

Your first step might be deciding on a script with your partner, if you have one, and then telling your children what you can and what you already know, even if you still don't feel *entirely* ready. This is the healthy way to begin overcoming your fears. You want love and honesty to go together and to grow together in your family. As Vangelisti also found in her research, people's decisions about whether to reveal a secret depend, in part, on their concerns about the well-being of the person at the heart of the secret, as well as their belief that the person to whom the secret was disclosed had the right to know about it.[4] Disclosing shows your care and respect for your child, your partner, and your donor. It is a sign of the strength of your relationship with your child and your own self-confidence.

Parent-child relationships also set the stage for the relationships that a child will form later in life. A lack of communication about the child's genetic origins can interfere with positive interaction among parents and their children. If dishonesty and its accompanying unease are embedded in the parent-child relationship, the children may grow up with an impaired capacity for real and open intimacy, thinking that a sense of separateness is normal, even in close relationships.

WHY DON'T YOU WANT TO TELL YOUR CHILD?

- My child is experiencing a normal childhood, but that will all stop once she knows about her conception.

- I am reluctant to revisit feelings of shame about infertility, feelings that may have turned into shame about donor conception itself.

- I feel guilty that I haven't yet told, but I fear my child will become angry and reject me when she finally finds out.

(continued)

- I am worried that "telling" will change my family dynamic, particularly that my child might feel more connected to her genetically related parent than to me.

- I don't think my child needs to know unless the fact of her donor conception becomes important, such as for medical reasons.

- My partner and I disagree over whether to disclose.

- I worry that telling is not the end of the dialogue or the story and that I may be unable to answer my child's questions about her genetics or ancestry, so it would be better not to begin the conversation at all.

- Genetics are just not that important.

The decision to talk about donor conception with your child can be difficult, even if you value familial honesty. As you read this section, in which we explore typical hesitations and worries, you might want to highlight the points that resonate with you; at the end, make a list of any other concerns you've had. Once you've made the list, you can carefully think through how your not telling affects you and your child.

Bev's children were conceived with donated sperm, and she candidly explains why she has decided not to disclose:

IT IS SUCH A TOUGH *and personal call. My husband and I have decided not to tell our twins, who are now two and a half years old. We picked an anonymous donor because we decided from the beginning not to tell. To me they have a dad/father/caretaker who loves them with all his heart, and they have a huge extended family who loves them with all their hearts. Although there have been times when I have thought that perhaps we should be prepared to tell our twins, I know my husband won't change his mind, so I ultimately don't feel it's a door that needs to be opened. We will be smooshing the donor's medical and family history into my husband's so they will know all that we know (and since he is anonymous, all that we will ever know). Biology, to me, is just not that important . . . love and family are and my children have all they could ever need in those two departments.*

Bev's summary captures many of the reasons that people have decided not to tell, so let's unpack them.

Biology Isn't Everything.

We agree with Bev: love makes a family, and families can be (and are) formed without a biological connection. On the other hand, many families choose donor conception precisely because they want to have a biological connection to their child. By negating the importance of such connections, parents hypocritically pretend that biology just isn't important. This warps the family history and the child's identity development. Imagine if Bev had instead adopted the twins; would she even consider not telling them that they were adopted? For decades the adoption world has counseled parents to be open with the adopted individual; in fact, today the birth and adoptive parents are likely to have met each other before the adoption occurs.[5]

Bev's downplaying the importance of biology may be grounded in unacknowledged fears that the children will not accept her husband as their father. And indeed, fear of rejection haunts almost all parents deciding whether to tell children about their donor conception. Parents worry that their children will feel differently about them and their partner once they learn that they do not share a genetic connection. Even the genetically connected parent may worry about how children will respond to finding out that their parents used donor sperm or eggs. They fear that their child will become emotionally distant or start looking for a replacement parent.

If you are scared of your child's potential reaction to the lack of a biological bond with one parent, then you need to focus on what that fear really means: Do you think you (and your partner) are not your child's "real" parents? Of course not. Instead, drop your defenses to achieve the open emotional state necessary for acknowledging and honoring your child's needs. Work on your own feelings so that you can face the situation honestly. Celebrate being a parent, and cherish the incredibly rewarding candid and honest relationship you will be building with your child. Recognizing that a biological connection could be important to your child doesn't negate, or even threaten, the bonds you have already created with your child.

I Don't Want to Open a Can of Squiggly Worms.

You worry about what your family and community will think if they find out that you were infertile and had to use donor sperm or eggs. Some religions are quite critical of these decisions. You worry that telling your child will create too many unanswerable questions for her, causing unnecessary pain. Guilt, shame, and fear can be paralyzing. If you are feeling guilty about "the secret," if you are ashamed of your infertility, or if you are afraid of your child's questions, then no wonder you haven't disclosed. But you can take control over the disclosure process. As donor conception has become more common, communities have become increasingly accepting of its use, focusing on the joys of creating new families. Family members already love your children, and this new information should not affect that love. And finally, as we discuss later in the book, you can help your child work through all of their questions. By telling, you are not opening the proverbial can of worms, but you are opening the door to honesty.

My Partner and I Disagree.

Two-parent families come with two personalities, so even if you've sorted out your own issues and overcome your doubts, your work may not be through. Your partner may still be unsure about telling, or may even be vehemently opposed to telling. It is very difficult to feel torn between the needs of different members of your family. You love your partner and your child and want to do what is best for each of them, even now, when those needs seem to be at odds. If your family has "protected the privacy" of the donor and "maintained the secret" from your child up until now, this difference in opinion between you and your partner is probably already a source of conflict in your relationship.

While disclosure is virtually inevitable in LGBTQ families, the parents may still have fears about what this will mean. In lesbian families where donor sperm was used to conceive, while both parents might have hesitations, the nonbiological mother may feel insecure about her lack of genetic connection to her child. Like the heterosexual father of a child conceived with donor sperm, she may be resistant to acknowledging the importance of the donor and fearful that her child will search for him, threatening her role in the two-parent structure. Similarly, the gay male partner who is not the biological father may dismiss the donor's role, even as he welcomes a relationship with a surrogate.

You need to start by speaking with your partner lovingly and respectfully about your feelings, concerns, and fears. This may not be easy, particularly if this is not the first time you've disagreed on this issue. If you're the type of person who thinks better with written scripts, then you might even want to write an outline in advance of your conversation to make sure that you cover what is important to you. Explore why this issue is so important to each of you, and don't be afraid to unearth any of the emotions underlying how each of you approaches disclosure. The decision to tell or not to tell, and when to tell, may have huge symbolic importance about how you each view your family. If you have truly reached gridlock, then you might want to speak with a counselor to help you work through this issue, particularly because it might be related to other aspects of your relationship.

Otherwise, continue talking. Your conversation should probably include helping your partner take a good look at whether he or she has sufficiently dealt with the grief of not being able to give your child a genetic connection. When this grief is not verbalized, validated, and fully processed by both parents, every member of the family can suffer. Throughout these conversations, be sensitive and aware of your partner's potential reservations. Some nonbiological parents fear that their kids, post-disclosure, will look at them differently and even subject their parenting to harsh scrutiny. They worry that they will be viewed as less of a parent and that their children will become closer to the parent with whom they share a genetic bond. As a tearful father told us, "Knowing that I don't have a biological connection with my child, I wanted to be the perfect parent, because that's all I have"—what an enormous amount of pressure for anyone to handle!

While reminding your partner that *all* mothers and fathers worry about parenting, and that every healthy child goes through periods of rebellion, gently insist that it isn't all about how you feel as parents: focus on your child's needs. The necessary change of perspective for the nonbio-logical parents is to go from a self-focused "I am not able to have a genetic child" to a child-focused "What does my child need and deserve in regard to knowing the truth?" Ask your partner to focus on your child's inborn interest in knowing about her origins, even if she has not yet expressed it. We all want to know where we came from, and your child's reality is that she is donor-conceived. This truth belongs to your child; let her have own-ership of it.

Make sure your partner has considered the potential complications of withholding the information from your child. Remind your partner that if you decide to tell your child at a later age that she is donor-conceived, or if she finds out by accidental disclosure, she is likely to be angry or feel a sense of betrayal at having had the information withheld. You may ulti-mately cause a great deal of pain, confusion, and anguish in your child. Is that a risk worth taking?

Let your partner know that not telling risks your child feeling angry toward *both* of you. In fact, your child may even feel more anger toward the biological parent, expressing compassion and empathy for the other parent who was not able to provide that genetic link. In a 2009 study, that's what researchers from Cambridge University and the DSR found about children who had been conceived through sperm donation and had heterosexual parents. They found that while children often felt sympathy for their fathers, they were more likely to feel anger toward their mothers for lying to them.[6]

Try to convince your partner to tell your child as early as possible. Ex-plain why this is so important: if you can tell your child at a very young age in a matter-of-fact way, the reality of donor conception will not be a significant issue in your family life but something that has been present from the start. It will simply be a part of your family story, like how you and your partner met or the time baby took her first steps. Offspring who learned the truth later in life more often report having negative feelings regarding their donor conception than those who learned at an earlier age. More and more, parents report that they believe it is important for the child not to think of the moment of disclosure as a significant event, equivalent to an "aha" or "coming-out" story, but rather as a part of growing up that is just not a big deal. Disclosure is much more easily tackled as part of the fabric of their ongoing development.

My Child Will Never Suspect, So There's No Reason to Tell.

Of course, the type of family affects both the likelihood of disclosure and the age of disclosure. In LGBTQ families, disclosure is likely to occur earlier because part of the necessary biological equation is obviously absent. Even before they begin to understand where babies come from, children in LGBTQ and single-mom households will ask why other children have dads or moms and they don't. For most of these parents, the telling itself will be less troubled and fairly straightforward; children will not be surprised, even if one or both of the parents remains somewhat uncomfortable. In a large study of donor-conceived people, three-quarters of those raised by single parents or lesbian couples had "always known" of their origins, compared to less than a quarter of those raised by coupled heterosexual parents.[7]

Heterosexual families are more likely to keep the "secret" because their use of donor gametes can more easily be hidden. But don't be tempted. Hiding won't protect you or your partner, and it is not good for your child. Even if the initial telling looms large, focus on the long-term goal of openness and honesty in your family. Think about whether it really matters to keep the secret that you used donor eggs or sperm. Realize instead that what really matters is your beloved child.

REASONS FOR DELAYING OR NOT TELLING

Yes, there are extreme situations that call for delayed—or even no—disclosure. Psychologist Diane Ehrensaft says that one of the circumstances in which parents might do well not to disclose donor conception "has to do with a child's fragility or vulnerability."[8] If your child has mental or physical difficulties, she may not ever be ready to cope with the story of her origins. When a young child is struggling with leukemia, or in the hospital with a serious illness, talking about donor conception may not be the most urgent discussion you want to have with her. Waiting would certainly be appropriate in circumstances like these.

On the other hand, children with mild developmental disabilities can often process the story of their origins, and, as with any other child, telling remains the appropriate path.

Yes to Telling

There are many reasons to conquer your fears and tell your children about their origins. Most fundamentally, you want to be open and honest and respectful of your child and his needs. Your wish is for him to grow up strong and confident in his identity. Speaking and seeking truth in donor families fosters healthy relationships and self-esteem. Truth should be the foundation for all interactions and shared experiences among family members. As parents, we expect the truth from our children; *they deserve it from us too.* If we want our children to respect us, we must show them that we respect their need to know their personal history. When a child knows the truth about being donor-conceived, he can relax in his family's secure, comforting love even as he expresses curiosity about his ancestry, medical background, and unknown donor family.

Perhaps most convincingly, studies of both donor-conceived people and adoptees support the decision to tell, and donor-conceived people have made their voices heard loud and clear: early disclosure is the best way to go. Even if parents never discuss donor conception, children often sense that there is an invisible elephant in the room. Growing up is hard enough without the added worry of invisible secrets.

Once you decide to tell, you are the one who creates and delivers the conception story, setting out that all-important script for her. (We talk about that script in the next chapter.) You don't want her to find out by accident so that someone else is in control of this story. Instead, you can celebrate her birth together. As a parent, you will rest easier knowing that you have delivered the truth in the manner that you felt was best for your child.

You can follow the straightforward path of honesty with clear directions on how to tell—and there is a significant emotional reward to following that path.

Your children need you to help them safely negotiate learning about their biological selves. Be careful not to project your own fears and hesitations onto your child. Your child will accept that you are her parent and the donor helped you become her parent. Therapist Susan Frankel reminds us of the importance of focusing on the major differences between active parenting—which you are doing—and donating eggs or sperm, not on your insecurities about your child's loyalties.

Yes, your children may struggle at times with not knowing about their ancestry or medical backgrounds, but you will be right there with them to provide whatever support they need. In counseling donor families, Wendy found that sharing these uncertainties and developing a plan for dealing with them often brought families closer together.

Protecting against Accidental Disclosure

Whatever your intentions, keeping the secret might be very difficult or even impossible; accidental disclosure is a real risk. Widespread secrets are certainly more difficult to keep. Even if they don't ever intend to tell their children, parents often tell others, such as family friends or relatives, about their infertility and use of donor gametes, and these people can then tell others. Professor Ken Daniels, who established the Social Work Department at the University of Canterbury in New Zealand, and his colleagues found that almost two-thirds of parents who had not told their children had told someone else.[9] Whether family member or friend, that someone else may spill the beans for you.

When offspring find out about their donor conception from people other than their parents, the revelation can be unnecessarily confusing and painful. One man found out from his "drunk Aunt Sally," who blurted out the secret but didn't remember doing so the next morning. Another woman overheard her mother on the telephone, begging a friend who knew the truth not to reveal it during an upcoming visit because "it would break a lot of hearts if it got out"; the mother denied that her daughter was donor-conceived when confronted afterward. But the daughter knew. Many times, the truth comes out during a family argument or a divorce, when tempers are running high and one parent wants to hurt the other. Bruce was extremely hurt by how he found out: "Dad got into a fight with his new wife, who then exacted revenge on him by calling me to leave a voice mail stating that he was not my father." Whether disclosure results from carelessness or vengefulness, this is flammable ammunition to use on a child: the only way to render it harmless is to tell your child yourself.

Even if they aren't inadvertently exposed to the explicit truth, children pick up on more than we can imagine. Uncle Bob says, "Cindy, you have your father's eyes." Cindy sees her father glance at her mother, who then looks down quickly, feeling guilt or shame. Kids know something is up, even if they don't know the exact information being withheld. Many donor-conceived people exclaim, after finding out the truth, "I knew *something* wasn't right!" Some supposed that their mothers had been unfaithful. Many have said that they lived with knowing something about them was different, and they were simply waiting for confirmation of this feeling. Others don't find out until after one parent has died, when they are going through old paperwork. At that point, there may be no one around who can answer their questions.

Britta Dinsmore, a psychologist who specializes in women's issues, wrote about disclosure on a Web site maintained by Parents Via Egg Donation: "Accidental or belated disclosure can cause a tremendous sense of hurt, anger, and betrayal, which almost certainly impacts a child's attachment to his/her parents, and willingness to allow trust and intimacy in future relationships."[10] The secret can end up causing much anxiety for the child, even if no one ever acknowledges it.

Loose lips, found paperwork or electronic records, overheard conversations, or crazed family dynamics are not the only causes of accidental disclosure. Many donor offspring have found out the truth from blood or DNA tests. Some high schoolers have even figured it out from what they've learned in their biology class about genetics and how genes affect your blood type and eye color. As medical testing becomes ever more sophisticated, and as we learn more about the influence of our genes, donor-conceived offspring are increasingly likely to find out the origins of their conception.

The New Words on the Street: Tell Early

The trend among reproductive medicine professionals and counselors today is to support parents' decision to tell children that they are donor-conceived. The Ethics Committee of the American Society for Reproductive Medicine, for example, acknowledges that it is the parents' choice whether to tell children but also notes that disclosure is "encouraged." Social worker Ellen Sarasohn Glazer, the author of *Having Your Baby Through Egg Donation*, supports disclosure even more strongly, calling it "essential." This trend is unsurprising, given that studies and experience clearly show that children benefit from an open discussion of their donor status—preferably as early as possible. In the somewhat comparable context of adoption, psychologists have shown that it is helpful for parents to be open with their children about adoption, including providing any information available about the biological parents.

Psychologist Patricia P. Mahlstedt and her colleagues examined mental health issues among people who learned at different points in their lives that they were donor-conceived. They recruited eighty-five participants using contact information from Internet-based support groups for adults conceived through sperm donation.[11] They found that children who learned of their donor origins earlier in life had a more positive outlook on the means of their conception than adults who found out later on.

Disclosure at a young age has a generally positive impact on children's self-esteem as well. Donor-conceived offspring who are told at an older age often explain after the fact that they always knew something was off. Offspring told at later ages report feelings of betrayal that something so important was kept from them, as well as feelings of anger and loss. As one donor-conceived woman explained, "I didn't learn the truth about my conception until I was thirty. My parents kept the secret out of fear about how my feelings for my dad might change if I found out he wasn't my biological father. I was very angry with them for having kept the truth from me for so many years, and though I still love them, our relationship has been strained somewhat by this betrayal of my trust. I wish I would have known the truth all along."

When Cambridge University's Susan Golombok and her colleagues examined the mother-child relationship in donor families and compared the interactions between those who had and had not told their children about their conception, they found somewhat less positive warmth and sensitivity in families without disclosure than in families where children knew about their status.[12]

The Words from Parents

Parents who have told their older children report their own joy and relief in their new and more open relationships with their children.

Hard as it may seem at first, telling your child will actually be the easier path in the end. Once you overcome your fears, you can educate your child and your family about donor conception, empowering them and easing your community life. When you and your child are open about donor conception, your community will respond in kind. At six years old, Wendy's son, Ryan, would meet new people by reaching out for a handshake and saying, "Hi, I'm Ryan and I'm a donor baby!" Some of the adults didn't know how to respond. But Wendy felt confident of her son's strong, secure identity. This is important for children as they enter school and move through life.

HEARTFELT ADVICE FROM THE MOTHER OF A DONOR-CONCEIVED CHILD

"I hope people decide to tell before they enter into parenthood. Making the decision after the kids are born is so much harder. Not telling will come back to haunt you. . . . It's not a matter of if, but when. You feel the burden of keeping a secret from your child every time you look at her. Your child develops a medical condition and detailed family history is needed . . . these are not made-up scenarios. . . . I am trying not to be preachy and to respect your choices, but please consider all the possible scenarios. None of this diminishes your husband's role as dad nor yours as mother—unless you choose to let it do so."

The Words from Donor Offspring: Yes, Yes, Yes

If you still aren't sure you can summon the fortitude to tell, let the words of donor-conceived people bolster you. Wendy has spoken with countless donor offspring; overwhelmingly, they believe it is important to be told the truth about their conception at an early age. Regardless of whether they are told when they are young or later in life, so many offspring have emphatically said: "Please, please, please be honest with your child about their origins from day one. It is the right and best thing to do for us and for you. Help us be proud of who we are."

WHAT DONOR OFFSPRING REPORT

In surveys, on the DSR discussion boards, through phone consults, in face-to-face meetings, and in e-mail correspondence, here are some other things that adult donor offspring have said:

- The sooner you tell us about our means of conception, the better.

- Transparency is key.

- The story you tell us helps us understand and accept ourselves.

- We are going to be curious about where we came from, and we don't want you to be hurt by our curiosity.

- Knowing about our ancestry and medical histories is important to us.

- Finding out about our conception didn't make us feel any less like your son/daughter.

chapter three

How, When, and What to Tell Your Child

One of the hardest things to teach a child
is that the truth is more important than
the consequences.

· O. A. BATTISTA ·

ow what?

You've made the decision to talk to your child about donor conception. Whether you made that choice when you first began to look at donor profiles, when your kindergartener asked for help with her family tree, or when your high school biology student began to ask about his red hair, you've set yourself a worthy challenge. How, when, and what to tell your child are hard issues for many donor-conceived families.

No matter the age of your child, you need to remember that you are telling her the conception story because you want honesty valued in your family. Even if she's unable to absorb the information when you first disclose, she will be grateful for your openness later on. In this chapter, we discuss the different ways donor-conceived families tell their children about their origins. We give you advice on how to tell, the cornerstone of which is: *it's never too early*. Don't despair if you've already waited years, though—we also share ways of telling older children. It is never too late to start telling the story, although your conversations and your child's reactions will be different depending on her age and, of course, her personality.

Children of all ages should be given sensitive information, such as the story of their conception, in a warm, loving, protected family environment, with an attitude of acceptance and positive self-regard for who they are and how they came to be. "Telling" won't be a single event. It's an ongoing, unfolding conversation that becomes part of your child's understanding of herself. If you find yourself getting hung up on choosing the perfect words, take a deep breath and just keep going. Exact words matter less than your loving honesty. Follow the advice of social worker Ellen Sarasohn Glazer: "Each conversation offers an opportunity to become closer with your child, knowing that speaking the truth is much more important than 'getting it right.'"[1]

"When I had a daughter with donor sperm almost twenty years ago, I knew from the very beginning that I would tell her that she is donor-conceived as soon as possible, even before she could talk. I also knew that if I didn't start early, it would become much harder to have the conversation. I started by 'reading' her some picture books as bedtime stories. Once she started talking, I told her that a nice man had helped me have the baby I really wanted, and that I am overjoyed by who she is."

—*Lisa*

"I think the main reason that I am so comfortable with who I am and how I was conceived comes from the honest and loving way in which my mother approached the topic with me, at a very young age. She explained my conception as a blessing that was only possible because she wanted to have me so badly and because a wonderful stranger donated half of the ingredients she needed to make me who I am."

—Lisa's daughter, Allie

Preparing to Tell Your Child

Before you tell your child about his origins, consider these questions to help you work through what you will say.

1. How comfortable are you with your decision to use donor conception? Do you or your partner have any unresolved feelings about not being genetically related to your child?
2. Have you begun to think about how to tell your child and others about donor conception?
3. How will you react if your child wants to try to find her donor or half siblings?
4. How do you feel about the fact that your child may never find out about half of her genetic heritage?
5. Who else knows about your child's origins? Who else do you want to tell?

6. How will you figure out your script for your community, schools, doctors, and the rest of the outside world?

7. Do you want any support? If so, will you look to family members, the donor community, and/or therapists?

First things first. To ensure that your child is comfortable with the story, you, as a parent, must be as comfortable as possible with your choice to use donor conception. Many people's misgivings linger and affect what they say and how they tell the story. As one woman explained, "I never expected to have to go outside my bedroom to have a child. This is a loss."[2] If your child feels that her birth signifies defeat in any way, this is not a healthy message for her to hear.

When your child is born, if you start—or continue—to have feelings of loss and failure, don't surrender to a paralyzing negativity that can scar both you and your child. Instead, remember to take that deep breath, relax, and focus on the reality of your amazing child. Feelings of loss because of infertility or the lack of a biological child are certainly to be expected. Many people need considerable time to grieve not being able to give their children a biological connection. Most modern adults spend a number of sexually active years trying their best *not* to get pregnant, so the reality of infertility comes as an unpleasant shock. Even if you are a single parent by choice, you still may need to come to terms with having a child in a way that you had not anticipated. (Same-sex couples typically do not experience these issues.)

Many members of the donor community have worked through these feelings, so you can find support and empathy from them. Reach out to those who have walked this path before you. When coaching families on the Donor Sibling Registry, Wendy has found quite often that learning how others have dealt with similar fears and hesitations make people feel much more confident about moving forward. Finding out about families who have successfully made it through this stage can bring a great sense of comfort, community, and support. Hearing stories about how kids greatly benefit from openness and honesty will bolster your courage to tell the truth.

Telling Early

You can talk to children even before they start to ask about where babies come from. Some parents start telling their children the story of their conception while they are still in utero. Others begin when their children are babies or toddlers. As a 2013 study on egg-donor parents found, they remain concerned about telling their children at too young an age.[3] But as we know, children are never too young—nor too old—to be told.

Small children love to hear the story of their beginnings and often ask to have it repeated. Don't worry about having the right language or perfect terminology. Tell this story the way you always speak in your house, with the same tone and level of seriousness. If you start this conversation at the beginning of your child's life, the information simply becomes integrated into your relationship with your child, without fuss or fury. Your child embeds the story of her origins into her identity and her place in the family the way small children do so much—naturally. Just as picking up another language is harder the older we get, absorbing such sensitive information is far more difficult for older children, teenagers, and adults. For young children, though, it's likely to be quite effortless. As nineteen-year-old McKenzie explains: "I can't even remember one conversation I had with my mom about my conception because there were *so* many. She was always honest with me whenever I would ask questions. It was a progressive conversation we would have as my understanding of my origins became greater."

TELLING THE STORY

Main starting points for the story you tell your young child:

I (we) wanted to have a baby.

You need an egg from a woman and sperm from a man to make a baby.

I (we) didn't have the sperm (egg) necessary to help make you.

I (we) went to a doctor who had the sperm (egg) of a nice person who wanted to help us conceive you.

The best times to talk are calm moments, when you're not preoccupied or distracted. These are important foundational conversations and should not be conducted in haste. At first, young children need simple, short explanations, so go slowly, one sentence at a time, pausing to see if they want to ask questions. Follow your child's lead as to how much to say. It's a time for you and your child to bond and for your child to feel secure that you are right there with her. Presenting children's origins as a natural part of their life stories—which of course they are—produces the best results.

You can integrate the story of your donor into the story of "the birds and the bees" when your child asks where babies come from. In a single-mother or LGBTQ family, if you have waited to tell, you can have a special and separate conversation when your child asks why your family seems to be missing a father. Solo or partnered male parents can do the same when your child wonders why they don't have a mother. For young children, very short and simple conversations will suffice.

You can also, like Lisa, use children's books to introduce the idea of having a baby through donor conception, and then tell your own story after you've closed the book. Children tend to remember facts better when they are conveyed through stories. You can find many books that are appropriate for different types of families who have used donor conception and who want to tell the story to their children.

Parents might develop their own ways of explaining, based on what works best in their family culture (and their own skills). One mother wrote and illustrated a special, personalized storybook for her daughter, titled *Brittany's Beginnings*. Another mother, Lynn, made a scrapbook for her daughter, with pictures and short captions, documenting the entire process: pictures of the doctor, a copy of the donor profile, the first sonogram of her daughter, a description of coming home from the hospital, and then continuing her daughter's story up to the present. When she tucked her daughter into bed at night, Lynn frequently told stories from the scrapbook. Eight years later, when preparing for insemination for her second child, Lynn and her daughter both worked on the new scrapbook that would someday become her brother's.

Although there are comparatively few resources on how to make a scrapbook for a donor child, there is much more guidance on how to do so for adoptive families, so those suggestions, available on various Web sites and in adoption books, may be useful. For example, one article distinguishes among a scrapbook of family memories, a life book that documents your child's experiences, and a baby book that explores how your child joined your family.[4]

If it seems odd to be talking to a young child about issues of fertility, remember that you don't need to share *all* of the details. ("Just how did the donor produce sperm?" or "What did the doctor do to get the egg from the donor?" are questions that can certainly wait until later.) Children absorb only the parts of the story that are meaningful to them at their current age, and even if you give them lots of details, they simply disregard the information that is too advanced for them. When told about their donors, young children tend to ask very practical questions and usually show little emotional response. Whereas older children and adults will respond to this information by shuffling and realigning the components of their identities, small children will be mainly gathering facts.

TALKING TO YOUR YOUNGER CHILDREN

1. Tell them the truth, and give them as much information as they need—but don't overload them with too many details.

2. Listen. Make sure that you don't do all of the talking. Engage with them and ask them questions, like "What do you think happened next?"

3. Let them know how important this information is to you, and take their responses seriously.

4. Make sure they understand this is not a secret that needs to be hidden.

5. Encourage questions.

How Your Young Child Might React

Once this groundwork is set, your child will know that he can always come to you and ask questions, even when the answers are uncertain.

The sooner you start to give your child the information, the sooner he can start integrating it into his life. *Ideally, your child shouldn't remember ever being told.* When Wendy's son, Ryan, was asked, as a teenager, "What was it like when you found out that you were donor-conceived?" he looked perplexed and answered, "I don't know. What was it like when you found out that you had blond hair?" It was just a fact that had been integrated into his knowledge of himself at such a young age that he couldn't recall not knowing it. Your child will appreciate how the story of her origins becomes an organic part of your life together and, at the same time, is not a big deal for her to accept. Terry, who is now twenty-five, explains: "Personally, knowing from a young age, I've always viewed it as a positive, not a negative (that is, I wouldn't be who I am otherwise!). There are no feelings of abandonment or like something is really missing from my life."

Children vary greatly in how important this information feels to them and in their levels of understanding what it means. At this preschool age, your child may not have specific questions and may simply listen to the information and move on to his next activity. Some children show little interest for years, only much later entering a period during which they think about the donor or possible half siblings. Other children become very interested, asking why Mommy's eggs weren't good enough or wanting to know if the donor has a family.

Even if your child does not reintroduce the subject, you should do so from time to time, reminding her that this will always be an open and safe topic of discussion. Adoption therapist Sherrie Eldridge suggests questions that might reassure children to let them know that you welcome their thoughts, such as, "I wonder where you got your love for Mexican food. Could it be from your [donor]?"[5] Or you might observe, "You are such a good dancer. Do you think your donor loved to dance as well?" Continue to talk about all the different types of parents and families there are, pointing out the variety of ways that families are formed to help your child understand that there is nothing strange about her conception or her family.

As children grow older, the story should grow with them, increasing in detail as they are able to understand more. Expect the questions you are asked to change as your child develops. Your goal in telling your young child is to create an open environment in which your child feels confident about herself and her origins, and in which being donor-conceived feels as natural as coming into the world in any other way.

Telling Your School-Age Child

You may decide to wait until your child starts elementary school to tell him the story, perhaps hoping to initiate the conversation when he gets around to asking where babies come from. After your child turns six or seven, the conversation will likely include more details about reproduction. Your child is aware of the differences between boys and girls and may hear schoolmates talking about where babies come from. Once you start talking, your child will likely have lots of questions for you. This doesn't mean, however, that he'll be totally comfortable bringing his questions to you; after a squirmy opening, he may be grateful to you for starting the conversation yourself.

To help your child understand her origins, talk to her about different types of families. She might have friends whose parents are two women or two men or single moms. Maybe she knows someone who was adopted. But even if she does have peers in various family forms, she might still have classmates who tell her (with all of the assurance of six-year-olds), "But you *have* to have a dad!" Your careful and loving explanation of where she comes from can help your child understand that she should be proud of her existence and her way of coming into the world.

Many children are asked to make family trees in school. This can be a great opportunity to solidify the concept of family that your child does have. If you are a single parent, then you can draw your own tree that includes all of the details of your child's known family. If your child compares her tree with those of others from her class (or if you are using a preprinted form), then you can prepare her to explain the missing branch of the family tree to your child's schoolmates and teachers. It's important to talk to your child about what she feels comfortable saying to others about her conception. Some mothers or fathers suggest that children explain, "I have a donor dad [or a mother] who doesn't live with us." Others suggest that their children simply say, "I have a donor who we don't know." Some children might feel more comfortable saying, without any further elaboration, "That's just how my family is." These direct statements can satisfy her elementary school class and give your child a meaningful response to their questions. However you and your child decide to frame the conversation, a chat with your child's teacher beforehand will be helpful, particularly if you live in a community where donor conception is unusual. It's important that the teacher be on the same page when difficult questions come up in the classroom.

TELLING THE STORY

The form of your explanation will depend on the form of your family. If your child already knows the basic facts of reproduction, then this conversation will be easier; otherwise, you'll need to explain those as well. Don't be afraid to use the correct words rather than euphemisms, but do use language that is appropriate to your child's developmental level.

For SMCs: "I wanted to have you very much, but there wasn't a man I loved who could become your dad, so I went to a doctor to get the sperm of a nice man. He knew that there were people like me who needed his help to have a baby, so he gave his sperm to the doctor's office for me to use. The doctors helped put the sperm inside me, where it joined with my egg to make you. I never met the man who helped me have you, but I am so thankful that he could help me."

For female [male] couples: "Our family has two mommies [daddies] and no daddy [mommy], so we went to a doctor to get the sperm [egg] of a nice man [woman]. He [she] knew that there were parents like us who needed his [her] help to have a baby, so he [she] gave his [her] sperm [egg] to the doctor's office for us to use. The doctors helped put the sperm inside of me, where it met and joined with my egg to make you. [The doctors helped us use her egg and our sperm to help make you.] We never met the man [woman] who helped us have you, but we are so thankful that he [she] could help us."

For heterosexual couples: "Your dad had sperm [your mom had eggs] that didn't work very well so we went to a doctor to get the sperm [egg] of a nice man [woman]. He [she] knew that there were parents like us who needed help to have a baby, so he gave his sperm [she gave her eggs] to the doctor's office for us to use. [Either: The doctors helped put the sperm inside of me, where it met and joined with my egg to make you. Or: The doctors put the egg into a petri dish, where it met and joined with the sperm to make you. Then, the doctors helped put the joined egg and sperm (you!) inside of me so that you could grow in my tummy.] We never met the person who helped us have you, but we are so thankful for that help."

In any of these conversations, you can also add whatever details about your donor seem appropriate, even sharing the donor profile.

How Your School-Age Child Might React

Children's responses vary, and, given how well you know your child, you'll have a good idea of how to prepare for their reactions once you tell them. Children at this age are unlikely to be fazed by the news, once they are assured that it just won't affect their daily lives in any way. But, some children might feel curious about their unknown biological parent. They may wonder if they look like the donor, or if the donor ever thinks about them. They may wonder about others born from the same donor. Some children might listen and then walk away, seemingly uninterested or even "grossed out" by stories about reproduction. Your cornerstone conversation will be one to build upon for many years to come as your child moves through different developmental stages of processing the information.

QUESTIONS YOU MIGHT HEAR

What is sperm?

What kind of an egg?

How did the sperm get out of the man?

How did the egg get from the donor to you?

Did I grow in your tummy?

How did the sperm or egg get into your tummy?

What is a donor?

Did you meet the donor?

Can I meet him or her?

Be sure to have some answers prepared.

After the initial conversations, you can be guided by your child's development and ability to formulate questions. Just because a younger child seems to have fully accepted the idea of donor conception does not guarantee that she will always feel okay about not knowing more about her genetic roots. The most important thing you can do to help her process her feelings is to remain open, patient, and not at all defensive. Children can ask questions that might feel embarrassing to you, so you need to be careful to respond with the same grace and honesty with which you have answered other questions. You should also remind her that it is okay to talk about her donor whenever she wants and make sure she knows that you welcome her questions. You can, for example, let her know how grateful you are to the donor who made her possible so that she understands that you do not feel threatened in any way. As adoption therapist Sherrie Eldridge emphasizes, you need to show that there is a "non-competitive spirit" between you, as the parents, and the donor.[6]

Telling Your Adolescent or Adult Child

If you have decided to tell an older child, then it is completely normal to feel some apprehension about your child's potential responses, and you may be struggling with your own feelings about how this could affect or cause a gap in your relationship. In preparation, get comfortable with your decision; drive out your demons, if any linger, and think hard about your child's personality and how she might react. When you tell, however, focus on your child's reaction; this is no longer about you. Your conversation will depend on the quality of your family's existing relationships and communication practices, and it will also vary based on the context in which you begin the discussion. No matter who initiates the conversation, you or your child, *don't make donor conception sound like it's something to be ashamed of!*

As you tell, set the tone for how you hope your child will react. The impact of finding out about donor conception at this age can be quite strong for adolescents and adult children, and you need to acknowledge these feelings. But you also need to make sure that your child understands that this new information does not change who they are: they are still the same people they were before they knew, with their same place in the family. As you continue the conversation, you can try to lighten it up, pointing out that your child now knows why she and her siblings look different from you or your partner. You can jokingly mention that she was lucky not to have had the chance to inherit her dad's big nose. Or you can talk about how it's clear now why she is interested in math, since you were an English major who only took math in college because you were required to do so.

Don't worry about saying the wrong thing: just being honest and having the conversation is important. You probably won't be able to answer all of your child's questions, but make it clear that you are willing to talk about and answer all the questions you can. You can even say, "I'm here for *whatever* comes up for you." Emphasize that you will do anything and everything you can to get them the answers they are looking for. Focus on your child's curiosity and reactions rather than on your own feelings.

Your tone is important; even at this stage, children are still influenced by their parents' attitudes. Your approach will help them decide how to convey this information to family and community. Don't ask them to keep the secret that you have kept for so long. Secrecy implies that there is something to be ashamed of. This is their information, and they have the right to share it. For older children, sharing and talking with peers will be important as they process the information and redefine themselves. For adult children, they will also be talking this through with their own families, including significant others, spouses, and perhaps even with their own children.

How Your Adolescent or Adult Child Might React

Prepare for some degree of shock, grief, anger, and confusion. Your son may be angry that you made the choice not to tell, based on your own fears or shame. He may feel a sense of betrayal, not having known the facts of his life all along, or he may feel a sense of grief, as he now has to come to terms with the fact that there is no genetic connection between him and some of his family members. As social worker Kris Probasco and her colleague, Megan Fabian, advise nonbiological parents, your child's realization that he shares a genetic connection "with someone else, and not with you, may be a time of sadness for both of you. Be there for him. . . . Tell him that you are sad, too, that he is not genetically related to you."[7]

For those with teens, this stage inevitably involves learning how to separate from you emotionally, and they may use this information to help them do so. Separation is normal, and you need to remain anchored and available. Adult donor-conceived children may have even deeper and more complex emotions and feelings because they have been living under false assumptions for a much longer period of time.

A feeling of loss is normal as he integrates this new information into his sense of self and family, and as he lets go of ideas about family connections that he had believed to be true for his entire life, including his ancestry and medical history. As tough as this may be for your child, it is still his truth to have and to hold.

Children almost always want to know why you withheld the information. If you initiate the conversation, be prepared to answer the question "Why now?" Being honest means thoroughly explaining why you haven't shared this information before and why you are sharing it now. You might have felt as if you were protecting your children from feeling different, or you might have been worried that your younger children could not cope with uncertainty about half of their genetic background. Here, it is okay to say, "I didn't know how to tell you" or "I thought you weren't mature enough," or even to acknowledge that you were scared of your child's reaction. Perhaps your partner never wanted to tell, and the two of you have now separated, so you are no longer worried about imploding your family. It may be that, as your child approaches adulthood, you don't want him to worry that he will inherit your genetic diseases. For some parents, they just couldn't carry the burden of secrecy anymore. If your reason for not telling was your own sense of shame related to infertility, you'll need to be honest about that too. It's important that your child understand that your not telling was because of your own struggle, not because there was something inherently shameful about the use of donor gametes. Whatever your reasons, make sure you understand them yourself and feel prepared to share them. Therapist Susan Frankel advises: "It's important to take ownership of your decision to withhold the information, and the impact of that on your child. Do apologize, and hold your need to be forgiven for a while. Disrupting their need to feel whatever they may need to feel so that you can feel better will only slow repair."

Quite often, there is simply a sense of relief: *finally* things make sense. Your child may have always suspected *something* because he's never been able to understand certain personal traits in the context of your family, and finally knowing the truth may bring him a huge sense of comfort. Many of the things that never made sense before start to click into place.

In any event, your child most likely won't assimilate the new information right away. Give him plenty of time. He may need to explore his feelings for you and other family members, and then figure out whether he is interested in researching and contacting the donor and any half siblings that might be out there. This initial, potentially confused, reaction to disclosure will not last forever. Experience and recent research tells us that emotions about being donor-conceived change for a majority of donor offspring, and feelings of "confusion" diminish over time. In the end, honesty can only strengthen your healthy relationship.

Although feelings of confusion may not last, feelings of angst may. Being honest with your child will not fill the voids of missing information. Some donor-conceived people continue to feel a sense of loss and even feel angry, desiring more information about the parts of themselves that come from unknown sources and for the family they might never get to know. One young woman, Carol, explains: "I suppose I still feel profound loss around this issue. I feel there are gaps in my identity. Knowing I am donor-conceived has helped me understand why those gaps are there—but not having access to donor info means I have no way of ever bridging or filling those gaps. . . . Being aware of my donor-conceived status does help me make sense of why I never really felt very connected with my extended family—maybe helps me understand why I've never really felt like I fit in." And here's how Mark articulated his feelings: "I am not sad. I am angry that half of my life's information is hidden from me, and I have no say in it at all. Until you have been in my shoes, you just cannot understand." There are some donor-conceived people who will never find peace with the facts of their conception.

It is normal to feel concern about how your relationship may change after telling. Some parents look to their children for reassurance that they are not angry and that everything will be okay, but it's important to understand that your children might need time to process the information. A genetic connection they took for granted has been revealed to be false. They may wonder, "Am I the *last* to know?" On the other hand, your child may be as eager as you for reassurances about the security of your relationship.

Your kids are not going to stop loving you when they find out they are donor-conceived. They might, however, be angry that you have kept the secret. You need to acknowledge their anger and overcome it together. After all, even in anger they will be looking to you for reassurance that your family is fundamentally intact and stable. They can be comforted by seeing that their family life will continue on, just as it has always been. In fact, after weathering the revelation, some donor offspring report a stronger and deeper relationship with both parents.

Be prepared for your children, particularly older ones who are especially sensitive to their parents' feelings, to worry about hurting you if they display too much curiosity about their donor. In two-parent families, children might intuit that the nonbiological parent feels a little insecure. In single-parent families, children do not want to minimize how much they love their parent. Preempt this concern by letting children know that you can handle talking about donor conception and are always willing to do so. Check in with them periodically to make sure they are not withholding difficult feelings or emotions while pretending not to care.

Some offspring simply don't want to talk about donor conception; particularly at this stage in their lives, the topic can be awkward. Others genuinely don't have any questions or much curiosity; it doesn't feel like a big deal to them. In this case (just as we advised for people who told younger children), stay open to their feelings and emotions. They may be watching you to test out how comfortable you feel about further discussion. Commit yourself to bringing up the topic again to provide for safe exploration, in case it is taking them days, weeks, or months to process this potentially identity-altering information. (More suggestions on how to do this are in Chapter 5.)

Sometimes, a variety of conflicting emotions can occur at the same time. As a child is grieving for the lost genetic connections he thought he had, he might concurrently feel excited about the genetic connections that he has yet to explore. Will it be possible to meet the donor? Do I have any half siblings out there? He might want to immediately get to work on figuring out how to gather more information on this new, unknown branch of his family.

Adolescents and young adults are coping with many other changes in their lives as they grow into their identities. Even in the same person, curiosity ebbs and flows. There might be periods when the donor is a daily topic of discussion for months, and then your child may get busy with other things and drop it for a long time. Follow your child's lead.

QUESTIONS FROM ADOLESCENTS/ TEENS/ADULTS

These are some of the typical questions adolescents, teens, and adults ask, although you know best what kinds of questions your own children are likely to have.

Why have you not told me before now?

Who else knows?

What is my medical history?

What is my ancestry?

Why did they donate?

Can I find out more about my donor?

Can I meet my donor?

Who else am I related to? Can I find them?

The Wrong Message

Although there are many right ways to tell your children, there are also a few ways that are wrong at any age. You need to tell the story in a respectful way that reflects your own comfort level; you don't want to use it as a weapon, nor do you want to engage in damage control if your child learns the story from someone other than you.

One woman explains how she learned she was donor-conceived, showing how badly a parent can botch the telling:

> **WHEN I WAS SIXTEEN YEARS OLD,** *my mother told me, "The man you call dad is not really your father. Your real dad is a donor, a man I have never even met." I know that there were tears in my eyes, but my mother just kept going and didn't even look at me. It was really hard because my father wasn't even there. He was driving my sister to soccer practice. My mother never even brought it up again.*

So much went wrong here:

- The daughter is already a teen when she finds out. (While this is better than never telling, it is less than ideal, and the whole process of disclosure is undercut by what the mother does.)
- Only the mother tells the story, with the father unaware of what is going on.
- Speaking of being unaware, the mother seems unable to recognize her daughter's feelings.
- "Dad" is the man who has raised her, so it is wrong to say that he is not a "real" father.

Stories like this, which are filled with hurt and confusion (on the child's part) and anger (on the mother's part), show what you should be careful to avoid. Instead, make sure that the telling process is, in the words of clinical psychologist Diane Ehrensaft, "an expansive and positive experience."[8] She recommends that the story, whenever it is told, focus on the joy of being able to have a child: "We wanted so much to have you, and we found a way to do it."[9] You should not denigrate the value of one parent, openly or subtly; if you have a co-parent, then tell the story together. Nor should you trivialize the donor's contribution. Under such negative circumstances, telling is more likely to confuse and anger your child instead of bringing you closer together.

My Child Just Found Out He Is Donor-Conceived by Accident—Help!

Finding out inadvertently can mean many different things to your child. He may feel anger toward you, or sad about a lack of genetic connection with you or his other parent. He also may feel confusion about his own identity. Give him plenty of time and make clear your willingness to hear what he has to say. Confusion is normal at first but need not be long lasting. The way you handle this phase will have an enormous impact on its duration and on the unexpected disclosure's ultimate effect in your family.

Your child needs to adjust to the fact that he was living under false assumptions about his biological origins. Everything he understood about his genetic continuity has to be shuffled. This is not easy work for anyone, let alone a young person. You can best help him through this by respecting the entire range of feelings that he might be experiencing. This is not the time to protect your own feelings or to ask your child to do so. He will be exploring completely new territory, trying to make sense of donor conception while rewriting his past and present identities.

More important, in this scenario your child must make sense of the fact that this information was kept from him for so long. He might feel deceived, mistrustful, furious, and accusatory. In families with two parents, you can expect a child to have altered feelings about *both* parents. Again, you can best help him through this by frankly explaining why you did not tell him about his genetic origins and, crucially, by allowing him to express these feelings without your becoming defensive or distant. If you feel regret for withholding the information for too long, make sure to apologize very clearly to him for that, while you are explaining your reasons for having done so. Having him understand why you withheld the information is important, but even more important is for you to be honest about how you feel now and to express any regret that you might be feeling. In fact, the key to managing this difficult period is to stay as connected as possible, remain open to what your child needs to say or ask, and, ultimately, show him through your consistent behavior that you are the same mother and father who have always loved him and always will.

The Reactions of Others

Once you've told your child, consider how your disclosure affects those around you. Sometimes teachers, other parents, and new friends are confused by news of donor conception even when your child is not. Children might experience a variety of responses from people outside of your family: surprise, curiosity, neutral and matter-of-fact acceptance, judgment, or criticism. Donor-conceived people might also confront discomfort. While surprise, curiosity, and neutral acceptance are fairly easy to handle, negative reactions are more difficult. Even if you find people who are uncomfortable with donor conception, or who judge and criticize, you can turn their reactions into teachable moments for others and for your child.

When Ryan was around seven, Wendy went to pick him up at a birthday party. A huddle of moms chuckling in the corner waved Wendy over. They told her that Ryan had been telling "tall tales." Since this was not in character for him, she asked what the tall tales were: Ryan had just announced that his mom "has never met my dad." Wendy confirmed the fact that, indeed, she had never met his father. The dumbfounded moms obviously had no way to process this information. She didn't let them suffer too long; she explained that she had used sperm from an anonymous donor whom she had never met. The other moms, now looking a bit sheepish, ended up asking many questions; they walked away from that conversation knowing a lot more about sperm donation. A few days later, another mom from Ryan's class called Wendy to say that she'd heard about what had happened at the birthday party and that she was really grateful for Wendy's openness about Ryan's origins. She then confided to Wendy that although none of the other mothers knew, her daughter was also donor-conceived.

Depending on your community, you might feel judged by people who do not completely understand or approve of your choice to conceive your child in this way, and who are uncomfortable talking about it. Therapist Susan Frankel told us, "Even in liberal San Francisco, other parents were horrified that my daughter knew so much about sperm and eggs, but for our family, those were the facts of her conception, not a story about sexuality, as it was perceived." Isabel reported feeling disturbed by others' reactions.

MY SON TURNED EIGHT YESTERDAY. *Henry is a big kid now, as he tells me, and he's right; he is four feet four inches and too heavy to pick up easily. Eight years ago, he was about six and a half pounds and shorter than my not-so-long arms. The other day, Henry was in after-care at school. When I picked him up, I heard from the parent in charge that she had commented earlier that Henry looks like his dad. "Uh-uh!" he replied loudly. "I didn't come from his sperm." She thought it was cute, but also told me the anecdote, saying "sperm" under her breath. Is sperm really a bad word? The exchange left me wondering whether he was embarrassed by her reaction (he denied it) and whether he is going to end up being teased in some way because of his innocent openness.*

Take control by talking to teachers so that they can help your child feel accepted for who he is. You may not need to talk to every single one of your child's teachers, but this can be important, for example, when your child is asked in elementary school to make a Father's Day card. If your vacations have involved meetings with sibling groups, you might need to explain to a teacher why your child has so many siblings. Your honesty and your advocacy set a great example for him on how to be open and to advocate for himself. When your child sees that you have no hesitation talking honestly about his donor conception, he learns that there is nothing to be ashamed about or to hide. Your child will learn to be proud of his donor conception, and to understand that it is part of what makes him who he is. You can similarly be a role model in your straightforward discussions within your community. For example, you may want to share the information with Scout leaders or your religious leaders. Your child's comfort with the facts of donor conception will have a profound effect on your family and communities.

chapter four

So Now You Know: For Offspring

Truth rides a long road.

· EDWARD COUNSEL, *MAXIMS* ·

For those of you who have grown up knowing about your donor conception, it might not seem like a big deal. At times you've probably been filled with questions and curiosities about your donor beginnings and your invisible donor family. But you've probably also experienced stretches of time when other parts of your life took center stage, times you didn't think much about the way you came into the world or your genetic links.

If you have just found out that you are donor-conceived, the idea of donor conception and, more significantly, the fact that a truth has been withheld from you may be hard to come to terms with, mentally and emotionally. You should know that it is entirely normal for you to be experiencing a variety of emotions about being donor-conceived. Many offspring report working through sadness, anger, ambivalence, and curiosity—sometimes all at the same time.

Whenever you found out, learning about other people's experiences can be affirming of yours and can provide support and guidance. Like you, many others have grown up as donor-conceived people, and you may recognize yourself in some of their stories and sentiments. After talking to thousands of people through the Donor Sibling Registry, Wendy has seen just how powerful it can be to hear other people's stories and to read about how others have walked this same path before you. There is a commonality you share that can create a bond, even though you may have entirely different experiences. Reading about the other donor-conceived people in this chapter can help you learn more about yourself, grow emotionally, and become even more secure in your identity.

Growing Up, Knowing

Stacy, who found her half brother on the DSR and then had the opportunity to meet him in person on *Oprah*, shared with others on the DSR how loved and protected she felt because she has almost always known that she is donor-conceived:

I AM TWENTY-NINE YEARS OLD *and have known I was donor-conceived since I was five. As soon as I showed curiosity about "where babies come from," my mom sat me down and explained that she had wanted to have me so badly but didn't have a special man in her life to help her. So she was lucky enough to find a special donor who was able to give her half the ingredients she needed to make me who I am. She told me that I was special because of that.*

I grew up viewing it as something that not only made me unique (especially back then when it wasn't so common or talked of)

but also was a kind of blessing because I wouldn't be who I was other-
wise. I think growing up with that knowledge allowed me to fully ap-
preciate how much my mom wanted me and also let my views on
being donor-conceived grow up with me in a natural and comfort-
able evolution. I know every situation is different, so I am not here to
tell anyone what is right or wrong, just wanted to share my experi-
ence. It has been the blessing of living a full and happy life knowing
how I came to be, out of a combination of my mom's love and my
donor's gift.

For those of you like Stacy, your parents chose to incorporate donor conception into your life story from the beginning and you can't remember a time before you were unaware of this fact. You completely accept this as part of your identity, but you may still have many unanswered questions and feelings that you'll explore. After all, you can see where half your genes come from, but the other half remains more or less mysterious. For many of you, your parents have created an affirming and safe family environment in which you can ask any question and discuss any feelings. If you're feeling as though you need additional support, you can always go outside of your family to friends, to other members of your community, to the DSR to ask for assistance from Wendy, or to a counselor who is well versed in the matters of donor conception.

Even if you've always known, you still won't be able to make sense of everything that you are experiencing and achieving all the time. No one can trace every single one of her attributes and interests to someone else in her family tree. On the other hand, for donor-conceived people, more of your talents, personality traits, and medical issues seem to come from an entirely unknown source than they do for others who have grown up seeing both of their biological parents and knowing their extended families. Like many adopted people, you can experience what's called "genealogical bewilderment," which psychologist Diane Ehrensaft defines as "the lack of knowledge of part of their biological roots."[1] You may often wonder: Did this trait come from the donor? Did the donor have an anxiety disorder or other mental health issues? Did the donor struggle with addiction? Tyler, a senior in college, had never been interested in drinking alcohol; when his friends went to keg parties, he was the designated driver. He recently discovered that there was alcoholism in his donor's family, and he wonders whether he sensed in himself a propensity for substance abuse.

Even if you are quite secure in your identity, you may want to know more about your donor and your half siblings to round out your sense of self. Just because you can't clearly trace character traits to a particular person doesn't mean that you can't have a strong sense of self-identity and appreciate those parts of your personality that you have inherited from your donor. Ryan Kramer felt like a complete person who just didn't know where half of himself had come from. When he was thirteen, he wrote this:

THE TRUTH IS, *not knowing my father is not something I think about on a day-to-day basis. It's not that I ignore it, but having known it since I was only two years of age has made it a part of my life that I embrace and accept. Some offspring say, "I don't know who half of me is." That's absolutely not true for me. While indeed I don't know where half of me came from, I still know what it is. There are parts of me, both physically and emotionally, that I can distinctly pull out of my mother's side: things about my nose and eyes and hands, and also emotional resemblance. Once I have isolated all of these things, the*

*process of elimination shows me the side I obtained from my father.
So while I have never met my father, make no mistake, I do see him in
myself, in my brown eyes, in my love for math and passion for engineering.*

While acknowledging the reality of your donor as a real, living, and
breathing person, you may still have fantasies about your donor's personality, achievements, physical and mental attributes, talents, and personality. Some experts believe that the most powerful role model in a child's
life is the same-sex parent, so when that spot is vacant, it's natural for a
child to try to fill in the missing pieces. Many donor-conceived men who
were raised without dads report that, like many other boys, they emulated
superheroes and famous athletes in their childhood. Unlike other boys,
however, they not only believed that one of these superhuman figures
might actually be their donor but they also installed them as substitute
fathers and role models. Girls imagine that their donors are ideal men in
every way. If your parent used an egg donor, you might have fantasies
that she looks and sings like Taylor Swift or has the mothering capabili-
ties of Michelle Obama. You might think your donor would have made a
better parent than the one you have.

While fantasies about the unknown are part of every young child's life,
the reality is that donors are just regular folks: no superpowers, no knights
in shining armor, no American Idols, no perfect parents. The potential
pitfall is if donor-conceived people imagine their donor has superhuman
abilities, then they can expect to have these unattainable qualities themselves and feel disappointed when they don't live up to their own expectations of excelling at music, sports, or academics. Having realistic
expectations about your donor and what you may have inherited is
important.

Your Different Story

Being donor-conceived does mean that you have an "origins" story that is a little different from those of many of your friends. This doesn't mean that you don't love your family, that your childhood is unhappy, or that you yourself are different in any way from your peers. But you may feel that your origins story distinguishes you from your friends. Our society celebrates the genetic tie, even if we have become more accepting of families formed without biological connections. If your parent is a SMC, you may feel that you are missing out on what many of your friends have: two loving parents. When you begin dating, you may have a fear of becoming involved emotionally or sexually with someone you may be biologically related to; when you have children, you will inevitably wonder about their genetic heritage.

Even though you realize that your parents went through extraordinary measures to have you, and even if you cherish their honesty with you, not knowing your full history can have a significant impact on your life. Some people never get over their frustration or anger at not being able to fill in details about their ancestry and genetic background, and they are never able to "work through it." It can be extremely frustrating for them to know that the sperm bank, egg agency, or doctor's office has information about their genetic parent that they can't have access to and that their parents deliberately prevented them from knowing. This situation may never seem fair or just.

You'll be processing your feelings, and moving toward acceptance of yourself, of the role of the donor in helping to make you who you are, and of your parents' choices. Some people simply need more time before they can develop forgiveness of their parents and, ultimately, appreciation of the situation as it is. Both forgiveness and acceptance may not come overnight, and they may arrive in stages.

Learning the News Later On

"It's not about feeling unwanted or unloved. For me, it's two issues: first, why was I lied to (was told at age seventeen), and second, why can't I find out who I am? And for me, being loved and wanted is not enough. Because being loved and wanted doesn't answer those burning questions. So it's important for your parents to help you ask the questions, and then help you to find the answers to them."

—*Corinna*

If, like Corinna, you have just become aware at an older age that you are donor-conceived, this revelation has probably had a significant impact on you. Although some experience a certain relief and nonchalantly continue their lives, very few people are thrilled to find out they are donor-conceived—it's a jolt to what they thought they knew about themselves and their family. Shock, anger, confusion, hurt, surprise, relief, sadness, disbelief, and curiosity are all common initial reactions. You may wonder why your parents took so long to tell you. And if it was not their intention for you to find out, you may be angry at them for hiding your origins from you, and you may feel grateful to, or furious at, the person who disclosed.

Whatever the situation, you've likely been overcome by a whirlwind of emotions that can take years to resolve. That was certainly true for Tammie:

I AM A DONOR CHILD. *My mom didn't tell me 'til I was twenty-one. I always knew something was different; I constantly used to ask if I was adopted. I never felt a sense of belonging. However, I feel incred-*

ibly hurt because I wish my mom had told me sooner. The way she went about telling me wasn't the best situation either, and made me very upset. Everyone else always knew; it was a secret that was kept from only me. I am now almost twenty-nine and a recent parent myself. As I deal with my pain and anger, I find myself wanting to know more and more about who my "dad" is, even if it is just medical history, etc. I think if my mom had told me sooner, I might be more comfortable with the situation. It is rough not knowing who your "dad" is.

Tammie's recognition of her feelings of betrayal, her understanding of this shock to her identity, and her growing acknowledgment of her need for more information show how she is still trying, eight years later, to develop a healthy approach to her situation.

In order to move forward in the healthiest way possible, you'll need compassion and patience for, and from, yourself and your parents. You need time to process and integrate this new (lack of) information. As Diane Ehrensaft points out, "For donor offspring with anonymous donors, to be denied access to half their genetic history can not only create medical risk but be a trigger for anxiety and depression."[2]

You probably want to ask your parents lots of questions. Usually, the first question is "Why have you not told me before now?" As you process the fact of your donor conception, it's important for you to understand why it was hidden from you. Many parents thought they were following the most sophisticated professional advice, the accumulated wisdom of the medical industry, when they were advised not to tell. It might help offspring sympathize with their parents' choices if they understood that the advice given to their parents was long considered correct, even though today that advice rings of archaic medical practices such as lobotomies.

So, it is important to stress that being donor-conceived implies that they were wanted, even if their parents didn't know the best way to handle disclosure.

Even for those parents who felt that telling was better (contrary to the advice they received), it may have seemed impossibly difficult, so they kept putting it off. Fear of disturbing a happy family life may have held them back. Sometimes parents disagree about telling, or the decision is left to the nonbiological parent, who may feel insecure about her parenting role and fear rejection. Your parents made the best decisions they could with the limited information and advice they had at the time. As is true of parenting decisions more generally, they believed they were doing the right thing for you. When many parents conceived, no one counseled them at the doctor's office and few talked publicly about donor conception. As discussed earlier, some courts considered it to be adultery if a married woman used donor sperm, even with her husband's consent, so mothers sometimes withheld the truth to protect their children. There were no media articles, no research publications, few books to read, and, of course, before the 1990s, there was no Internet.

The better you can understand why they waited to tell you, the more you'll be able to handle any feelings, such as anger, that you might be experiencing. Even in anger, try to let your parents know that you want and need their love and support, now more than ever. This may be a difficult time for all of you, but they are still the same parents who have always loved you, and you are still the same person who has always loved them. Ultimately your bonds with your parents can become stronger and deeper.

IN THEIR OWN WORDS:
COMMON REACTIONS TO FINDING
OUT AT A LATER AGE

☀ "I felt both elated about not having the possibility of inheriting my dad's health problems, excited to finally know the truth, confused about how this could even have happened, and very disappointed that both of them allowed me to live with a secret that was toxic to them and detrimental to my mental health."

☀ "I felt totally blindsided, sort of dumbfounded, speechless, confused but also that things were now very clear because in my heart of hearts since I was a child, I knew *something* somehow was amiss though I couldn't place what."

☀ "So sad that my dad was not my biological father. So, so angry that my parents had not been honest with me from the beginning. I felt like I didn't know who I was; my identity was shaken."

Some offspring are deeply saddened by what they feel as the loss of an important connection to one parent—the biological tie they had always assumed existed. The mom of Cody, a twelve-year-old boy who had just been told that his dad was not his biological father, reported that her son said he was "heartbroken" just after hearing the news.

But Cody's feeling of loss and Tammie's feeling of anger are not the only possible reactions. For a few, the new information is like water off a duck's back. They just take the news in stride: "I knew I was loved, I did not see the big deal." Counselor Olivia Montuschi points out that she also knows "some people who learned of their status as adults but who defy the stereotype of this being an experience that threw their identity into question and undermined trust in their family."[3] A very small number have even said that they thought it was probably easier to manage the knowledge as an adult and were glad that they "had not been told earlier."[4] Recognize, however, that your comfort with being donor-conceived may vary as you move through the different stages of life; having your own children or confronting your own first serious health problems, for instance, may bring up the issue again in unsettling ways.

Sometimes, when people discover that they are donor-conceived, everything clicks into place. They finally have an explanation for differences they have always perceived between themselves and one parent. This may be the case for you if you have always had a feeling that something about the family was "off"—maybe you looked different or had truly divergent talents or interests. Some people say that they never felt they had a genuine bond with their dad, as if the secret had slipped an unseen barrier into the relationship. Even in a close-knit family, you may have felt that something just wasn't right, picking up subtle cues from your parents or others who knew the truth.

Offspring who have lived with fears of inheriting the illnesses of a parent are relieved when they learn that, because there is no biological connection, they have nothing to be afraid of. Twenty-five-year-old Anne said that she felt a sense of relief when she learned that she did not share DNA with her father: he was an alcoholic with many physical and psychological problems.

You need to acknowledge whatever emotions this news has brought up for you. When donor-conceived people grieve for the loss of their presumed genetic connection to one of their parents, or for their absent genetic parent, or for the other genetic relatives they may never find, their sense of loss can be difficult for others to understand. Here's how nineteen-year-old Rebecca expressed her frustration at the denial of her feelings:

I AM VERY SAD TODAY, *with a grief that isn't supposed to be talked about. It is just not allowed. Because I had two loving parents, I am not granted that right. People ask, "What are you complaining about?" You were supposed to forget about your father, the man who gave his sperm so that you could come into being. You had everything. Why would you want more? "We gave you everything!" Yes, I did have everything . . . everything but my genetic father. You just can't fix that. I feel like a tree that has half of its roots missing. And without them, I can hardly stand up.*

Even though Rebecca really does love and appreciate her parents, she still experiences a profound need to find out about her invisible half. Although you might find it difficult to acknowledge these feelings even to yourself, you will find support if you reach out to the donor community.

While many people think about their donors, not all of them experience the same grief as Rebecca. Unlike some adopted individuals, most donor-conceived people do not feel as though they have been abandoned or "given up" by their unknown parents. As Gordon shared: "I don't have any sense of having been abandoned. I am very close to my parents, and I am not seeking my biological father because I lack a rewarding relationship with my father. I simply am missing some information about where I came from." As you know, genetics alone do not make a parent; the relationship is born of daily nurturing and care and love. Some offspring develop deep compassion for their nonbiological parent who wanted that genetic connection but never had it. They deeply appreciate and respect that parent's ability nevertheless to form a strong parental bond.

No matter what you're experiencing, have patience with yourself. Denying the complexity of your emotions can be self-destructive. Instead, you need to acknowledge your feelings so that you can begin to manage them, heal relationships within the family, and move forward with your life. If you're feeling grief, then accept those feelings. If you're feeling guilty about not appreciating your wonderful and loving parents because you are so angry, then acknowledge your reactions, understand that they are to be expected, and try to work them through: otherwise, this will only tie you up in more knots. Even if you are never able to complete your family tree, you can still move toward acceptance. Expect your emotions and feelings to be fluid. Sometimes, initial feelings of ambivalence may turn into curiosity, and confusion may turn into acceptance; negative feelings of betrayal or sadness can, in time, give way to forgiveness and even lead to exciting discoveries about yourself and your extended family.

Some of you may recognize yourself feeling one or more of the five stages of grief that Elisabeth Kübler-Ross famously identified in her book *On Death and Dying*: denial ("This can't be happening, not to me"); anger ("Why me?" and "Why did my parents keep this from me?"); bargaining ("If only this isn't true, then I'll be an even better child to my parents"); depression ("I'm so sad that I might not ever know my donor" or "I'm so sad that I'm not biologically related to one of my parents"); and acceptance. In this last stage, you acknowledge that life will never be the same but that you can and will live with this new knowledge. The anger or sadness will start to fade, you'll begin to heal, and you'll be able to reach out to those around you. You'll begin to integrate your new knowledge into your identity.

Talking to Family Members When You Find Out Later

Now that they know, some offspring want to talk freely to their parents about any aspect of donor conception. Others say that they're not comfortable discussing anything relating to their origins with their parents. They may want to protect their parents, or they may feel frustrated, misunderstood, and shut out whenever they try to talk: "I don't want to go into it with my dad because I don't want to hurt him," "I feel that curiosity about my donor might upset my dad or make him feel threatened," "My mom feels uncomfortable and defensive." If this describes you, persevere; remind yourself how important it is for you to find out where you came from and how much you want to be able to discuss this openly with your loved ones. You don't need to protect your parents from your questions. The more you progress with your new open dialogue, the more comfortable your parents might actually become. For some parents, it actually begins to feel good. They feel a great sense of peace in finally releasing the truth they have kept under wraps for so long.

Spend some time thinking about how to talk to your parents in a way that will be as comfortable as possible for all of you. This isn't about planning specific conversations, but figuring out how to have the freedom to talk about your feelings, medical issues, searching for information, and any other donor issues as they arise in your life. If you can, always begin the conversation in a nonconfrontational way, gently but clearly reminding your parents that this is about you and your interest, not about their parenting. If a question occurs to you and the time isn't right to ask about it, or you aren't ready, write it down and bring it up when it makes more sense to talk. Keep a growing list but don't let it get too long. The whole family will benefit and grow closer if you find a way to talk openly about this subject.

You'll probably want, and may need, their help in getting more information about your ancestry and medical background; for example, the clinic might only be willing to release information to your parents, the "patients," and not to you. You'll want to ask your parents how much they know about the donor and, if they didn't actually choose the donor, then who made that choice for them, and how. What type of information were they given at the time? Have they inquired about or received any other information over the years? Are there any updated donor profiles or medical information?

You'll also want to talk to your parents about issues of privacy and secrecy. They might have told you that very few people know about your donor conception, so you might say: "I want to talk about this with Aunt Debby. How much does she know?" This is your information to share or to keep private. Your decision on how, and with whom, to discuss your origins is personal. Make sure that your family understands your wishes. Maybe you'd like to keep this information to yourself for a while, as you process through it. Or maybe you're ready to tell the world—and if your parents haven't been, then they will have to adjust to this new openness.

UNTIL YOU FEEL COMFORTABLE TALKING WITH YOUR PARENTS, SEEK OUTSIDE RESOURCES.

*   Talk to other family members and friends.

*   E-mail or set up a phone consult with Wendy Kramer.

*   Connect with a counselor who works with donor-conceived people through the DSR's Web site.

(continued)

> ☀ Read about others on the DSR Web site who have experi-
> enced similar feelings, and, if you choose to do so, con-
> nect with them.
>
> ☀ Search for other online chat groups for adult donor off-
> spring whose experience and approach are similar to
> yours.

Redefining Yourself

As you incorporate donor conception into your identity, you may notice
that you spend more time in front of the mirror, wondering who else out
there shares some of your physical attributes. One woman said, after finding out she was donor-conceived: "Looking in the mirror was strange. I
felt like I was not the same person. Suddenly, everything looked different
and there was a new angle to look at myself with. It felt like there was
something or someone else looking out of my eyes back at me. It was like
something had shifted."[5] For many, the desire to see these mysterious and
unknown qualities reflected back in another's face will prompt them to
move forward with searching for their half siblings and donors.

You might also have concerns about health issues. Until now, you
thought that both parents' medical histories mattered to your own medical
future. You may have had screenings, based on a parent's illness or medical history, that you now realize were unnecessary. For example, after
your dad's heart attack, you rushed in for a heart screening, worried about
whether you inherited his cardiac condition. Or you may have medical
issues that don't correlate with anyone in your family, and now you know
why—and wonder what else may lurk in the missing half of your ances-

try. The dermatologist may have asked you if there was any skin cancer in your family history, as she decided whether the birthmarks on your skin should be checked every year. Now you may wish to make those yearly appointments because you cannot know for sure that skin cancer was not an issue for your unknown biological parent.

And, as you think about dating someone, talking about donor conception is important early on. Being donor-conceived might be something you bring up on a first date—or you might not feel comfortable mentioning it until you have established a slightly more serious relationship. Ryan always knew that if he was interested in dating someone, he would need to ask if she was donor-conceived; if she had been, they'd need to swap donor numbers. Since many offspring don't know they are donor-conceived, if the relationship does become more serious, it is important to probe the other person's origins. This could mean asking your date's parents directly—not exactly the small talk most young people are accustomed to making—or, at the very least, letting your date's parents know you are donor-conceived.

Telling Your Community

It can be hard to know how and whether to tell other people that you are donor-conceived. Who do you tell? Family members? Friends? Your doctor? Should you reach out to other donor-conceived people, just to talk about what you're going through? If you do start to talk about donor conception, your family members and friends will probably need time to get comfortable with it. They are likely to ask questions that you may be unable to answer. This is not to discourage you from talking: as they overcome any uncertainty or uneasiness they feel, the members of your support network will help you work through your feelings and establish a "new normal" for your life.

OTHER PEOPLE'S REACTIONS ACCORDING TO DSR OFFSPRING

☀ "Most people think it is awesome and are surprised. It's a part of who I am and I am more than at peace with it, so it's not difficult for me to talk to anyone about it. If it makes people uncomfortable, they don't need to be a part of my life."

☀ "With doctors, it is difficult—having no medical history of the donor. Also with my twin brother, who refuses to discuss and does not want anyone to know. Also most of my family members do not know and that does not feel right to me."

☀ "I don't like feeling different. When I tell people about it, they always say I am the first person they have ever met who was born that way. Honestly the biggest thing for me was not a having the role model most kids get with a father around. Because of this I had to look around for male role models."

☀ "While I've never had people make an issue of it because I share it with so few individuals, I hate the constant questions about where my father is. I'm bombarded with these questions, and I feel like sharing the story of my conception would only bring about hundreds more. While I don't mind this with people I'm close to, I really wish donor insemination were more well-known and commonly accepted."

You can control how others will perceive your donor conception. They will look to you to see how you frame your origins story: Is it the major tragedy of your life, is it an exciting part of who you are, or is it simply a fact about you that doesn't come up in everyday conversation? The more relaxed and confident you are with your donor conception, the less of an issue it will be for anyone you choose to share it with. It will simply be integrated into their idea of you and your personal story. If you are emotionally at ease when you talk about it, others will likely respond in kind.

And Just What Do You Think about Donor Conception?

Many donor-conceived people feel gratitude to the donors who helped make their lives possible, and some even use donors themselves when they start families, but this gratitude and acceptance is not universal. You may feel conflicted and angry about the whole practice of donor conception, like Eric: "It makes me angry that my parents thought it was a good idea to pay a stranger for his sperm, and then to bring me into the world being denied the basic right of knowing who my father was and what ethnicity I am." There are some donor offspring who feel strongly that donor conception should be outlawed, saying that it is not right to bring children into the world who will have no hope of knowing about their ancestry or genetic backgrounds. They point out how strange it is that the genetic connection between parent and child is honored and valued in our society, whereas the genetic connection between child and donor is often dismissed as unimportant in the world of donor conception. They note that the loss of kinship, the increased complexity of identity formation issues, the lack of genetic health history, and the dearth of heritage and culture are tough to bear. And for some, the thought that their biological parent so easily sold their genetic heritage is extremely discomfiting. They wonder, "How could a person sell their gametes and live with the knowledge of having countless children out in the world, children they'll never know about and take responsibility for?"

"My feelings are difficult to explain to people who take their roots for granted. An adopted person once described the sensation of genealogical bewilderment as having to drive through life without a road map. I find it to be an apt description of my situation. People who know both of their biological parents find it hard to grasp the enormity of what I am missing. Simply having information about the sort of people they are, and what things they are capable of doing, is comforting in a way that you can't understand unless you've actually lived without it."[6]

We have never met anyone who wished that he had never been told he was donor-conceived. Even an uncomfortable truth beats out the seemingly blissful lie that negates your identity. As you come to terms with your own origins and as you learn more about your parents' motivations, you will develop your own approach to the ethics of donor conception. And for most, you will now embark on the next part of your journey— finding out how much and what information exists on your donor family.

chapter five

After the Telling

In all of us there is a hunger, narrow and deep, to
know our heritage, to know who we are and where
we have come from. Without this enriching
knowledge, there is a hollow yearning. No matter
what our attainments in life, there is a vacuum, an
emptiness and a most disquieting loneliness!

· ALEX HALEY ·

D isclosure is just the beginning. Your child has the rest
of her life to decide what to do now that she knows. Chances
are that she'll want to learn more. Like many donor offspring, each
time she looks in the mirror, she'll wonder whose eyes she has, or, whenever she plays a note on the piano, she'll be curious as to whose musical
talent she's inherited, or whenever she goes running, she'll be worried
about whether heart problems lurk in her future. It is only natural for a
donor-conceived person to want to fill in the gaps.

As you and your children explore the meaning of donor conception, they will have lots of questions for you. They may even ask the same questions—over and over. If you are a parent, then welcome any and all questions: they are signs of the strength of your relationship and your child's trust in you. Your child is looking to you for comfort, support, and information. In fact, your child needs to be reassured that his curiosity and desire to know more about his donor, and perhaps to search, are entirely normal and won't hurt you. You can be curious and even a little excited and scared together. *How you manage this dialogue can set the tone for the relationship that you'll have with your child for the rest of your lives.*

Now that your child is asking questions, you'll be dealing with all kinds of interesting situations. Let's explore some of the more common scenarios that families experience as they talk about and process their questions and curiosities. While knowing that you are donor-conceived from before you can remember is quite different from finding out later in life, all donor-conceived people may walk through life with many unanswered questions. Family dynamics, relationships, and communication skills come into play as families handle these uncertainties in their own unique ways.

Making Space for Conversations

Your refraining from judgment gives your children the freedom to express all of their conflicting emotions. Parents should, if necessary, create opportunities that show how comfortable they are with donor conception. Yes, your children may find it awkward; they may even cringe when you mention the donor. Even if they're feeling angry that you didn't disclose earlier, you need to reassure them that you're ready to talk when they are.

Supporting your child's curiosity means that you need to talk openly about her donor. This gives her permission to continue talking as well. If you don't, then your child may think that the donor is not a person to be acknowledged or discussed, and, if you appear to be uncomfortable, she may actually feel shamed just by being the donor's child. When you ignore or negate the donor, you are ignoring or negating half of your child's existence. Recognizing that "invisible half" of your child is important. Again: Be proactive in talking about the donor. Sit down with your child, review with her the donor profile and any other information you might have, and don't be afraid to talk about the parts of your child that came from the donor. Continuing the conversation helps your child feel more comfortable with her origins, prompts her to ask questions, and moves her toward ownership of this information. Use these conversations to support her development. Whenever Ryan learned of a new talent or interest, he and Wendy would pull out the donor profile and read through it to see if perhaps his donor, or anyone in the donor's family, had the same abilities or interests. Regardless of whether he saw this new talent reflected in the profile, Ryan found the process of looking for connections with the donor to be comforting in helping him better understand himself.

In fact, you can be infinitely creative in making and finding spaces for exploration. When you're at the doctor's office talking about your child's medical history, help your child understand what this means. If you read stories in your child's classroom, ask your child and the teacher if you might read a book about donor conception. On your child's birthday, or on Mother's Day or Father's Day, you can encourage her to write a note card, letter, or journal entry to the donor to share with you. These activities help your child articulate her feelings toward the donor, and they give you a window into your child's emotions. You will better understand exactly what it is that your child wishes her donor could know about her. Even if the donor never sees the letter, it can be therapeutic for your child to express her emotions and curiosity. If you do this annually, you can keep the letters together, perhaps in a scrapbook, as a way of recording your child's thoughts about the donor. You and your child can read and reread the letters together over the years, tracking her changing questions and feelings.

"To celebrate Father's Day, my daughter and I listened to the audiotape we have of her donor speaking about life and choices that was provided by our sperm bank. At twelve, my daughter is finally able to relate to the tape and understand a lot of what her donor is saying. She's heard parts of the tape before, but today was the first time she connected with the person on the other end. She pointed out similarities in their beliefs, was excited to hear about his interests, and pondered the 'nature vs. nurture' theory. She was excited to hear him speak with such intelligence on topics she herself is interested in. She wondered if someday she would be like him.

"Because she has known about the donor since she was old enough to understand she had no daddy, she is comfortable with all aspects of her creation and her life without a father. Although it would be wonderful to see them able to connect at some point in time, for now she is happy being who she is, and knowing that a nice, wise, creative man took the time to make sure she had a chance to live. Happy Father's Day to our donor!"

My Child Wants More Information Than I Can Provide

Although you probably have the donor profile and maybe even a baby picture of the donor, you may not have other information. Ryan asked

Wendy about his donor at a young age. But since she had been assigned an unknown donor from an unknown sperm bank through that "nice lady behind the desk" at her fertility center, she initially had no information whatsoever about the man who had contributed half of her son's DNA. Many others who utilized donor conception before the 1990s, or from other countries, will find themselves in the same situation.

If you do not have much donor information to share with a curious child, be candid about what you know and don't know. If you can't provide specific information in response to a question about the donor, then here's a great way to respond: "That's a really good question, but I don't know the answer. I wish I did. Maybe we'll be able to find out. Should we start looking?" Your child then clearly understands that you're telling her everything you know and that you're not hiding anything—and that you'll always be next to her, searching for the answers to her questions. While you might feel insecure because of your lack of knowledge, she'll see your honesty as a sign of strength.

If he is interested, you can tell him that you will help him collect more information. Even if your child is not ready for contact, you can still gather additional information about your donor and any potential half siblings. The DSR should be your first stop and it can fill in some details. You may see other families who have posted on the DSR for your donor and learn about the ages of other half siblings, levels of contact desired, types of families, and medical conditions. You may even be able to look at photos. Many families, and even donors, post personal messages about themselves for other genetic relatives to read, so just reading through their DSR postings and personal messages gives you and your child many more details and can help satisfy her curiosity.

You can also remind your child that you actually both know quite a bit about the donor because of who your child is: talk about the parts of your child that don't appear to come from you or your side of the family. Sometimes this process of elimination will allow both of you to imagine the donor in a more realistic way; this was the case for Ryan and Wendy.

My Child Has Complex Feelings

Denise found out when she was twenty-one that she was donor-conceived. Having never questioned her closeness to her family, she was somewhat disturbed to learn that the younger sister she had always cared for so intimately was only a half sibling. But even with that revelation, her world was not shaken for long. "I guess I felt surprise, a little betrayed," she says, "but not truly different." Today, almost two decades after she found out, she explains: "I don't see my sister as my half sibling. She's just my sis."

Denise's story illustrates the movement from emotional complexity to calm (if curious) acceptance. Even though she now knows that her sister is actually a half sister, she has decided to define that relationship on her own terms. She manages to live with the "nagging" questions that so many donor-conceived people have about their genetic and cultural heritage: Who is it she looks like? What is his medical background? What is his nationality? Could her son accidentally marry a relative? "Would I like to know other half siblings? Absolutely! I think that is baked into our humanity," says Denise.

Acknowledge your child's feelings and find a way to enter her emotional and psychological worlds. Listen not just to her words, but figure out her state of mind. She is coping with another significant person in her life, someone whom she may, at different times, call "my biological mother," or "my donor father," and she is also struggling with how you, her parents, relate to the concept of the donor. Reassure your child that *you accept her feelings* about the donor and will follow her lead, including the language she uses to describe the donor. Use the same terms that she uses: you may still think of this person as your donor, but, when talking to your child, call her "your biological mother" rather than "my donor." While younger children are more likely to follow your lead, older children are experimenting with what the donor means to them.

Recognize that your child may not be fully willing to share all of his thoughts and may not accept them himself. For example, as you already know, many donor-conceived children have some fantasies about their donor parent, and they may be embarrassed to tell you about these fantasies. Tell him that his feelings are entirely to be expected, and let him know that donor-conceived people have many different feelings toward their donors, feelings that can change over time. There might be times when he goes for months without mentioning the donor, but then, around his birthday, he starts to ask lots of questions but turns his head away as he talks.

As you cope with his reactions, you may discover that you too still have complex feelings about acknowledging the donor as a real person with whom your child shares half of his genetic heritage. Genuinely accepting his feelings, and working through your own concerns so that you can support your child's curiosity about the donor may feel like a lot of work for you, but you need to do this for him. Just imagine the emotional work your child is undertaking as he grapples with his own thoughts and feelings about the person who helped to create him. Find ways to be brave and develop healthy responses to his natural curiosity. This sometimes difficult process will ultimately pay off in improved understanding of your child, the banishment of your own fears, and ever-better parenting.

As your child deals with feelings about her donor, another complexity may be her discomfort with talking about the donor to one of her parents—but not the other. Bonnie, a teenager, had hesitations: "For a long time I feared trying to learn more about my donor because I did not want to offend my father and make him feel inadequate." Various factors affect your child's willingness to talk. Her own personality matters, as does the type of family you have created: children seem to feel less comfortable in heterosexual families. In a study of 751 offspring, 84 percent of those with LGBTQ parents felt comfortable expressing curiosity about their donors with their parents, compared to 67 percent of those with straight parents. Those who didn't feel comfortable explained that they didn't want to hurt their parents' feelings or make them feel guilty. This was especially true in donor families with dads. (Egg donor children were too young to respond to this question.) Older children worry that their fathers will interpret curiosity about donors as criticism of them or of their parenting abilities.

Make sure that both you and your partner try to draw out your child's questions. If she is talking only to you, pull your partner into the conversation. Some children naturally gravitate to one parent for some issues (ranging from how to put on makeup to how to use birth control), but this is an issue that she needs to feel comfortable talking about to both parents.

My Child Wants to Meet Other People Who Are Donor-Conceived

Even if your child has no interest in seeking out her donor or potential half siblings, she might want to meet someone else whose parents used a gamete donor. You can tell her that there are probably many more than a million other people in the world born through donor sperm or eggs. If you have been part of a pre-birth support group and already know others who have used donor conception, this type of connection will be easy.

But you might not know of anyone in your immediate circles. Given our culture of secrecy, no one else in your community may ever have disclosed their use of donor conception, although, because of the high rate of donor usage, it is likely that you in fact already do know someone. You can find other donor-conceived individuals in a variety of ways. First, there are thousands on the DSR. There you can likely find people who used your sperm bank or who live in your area. Second, you might contact your child's teachers or a religious leader to find out if they know of others who have not disclosed more publicly. Third, you can approach same-sex parents with children in your child's class, as there is a good chance their kids are donor-conceived too. Finally, you can try asking your pediatrician to put you in contact with anyone else that she might know.

My Child Is Curious about Her Half Siblings

Young children may not consider or understand the possibility of half siblings, other children born from the same donor, until you bring it up. But it is often the first thing that occurs to older children after they are told they are donor-conceived: "Do I have any half brothers or sisters?" As fourteen-year-old Alison told her mother, "I think I would have something in common with these people immediately, and we all kind of share this missing piece in our lives of not having a connection to half of where our genetics came from, so it would be cool to meet them." The half siblings are not, of course, related to you (the parent), but they do share half their DNA with your child. The possibility of seeing that "invisible" side of themselves in someone else can be very important, and it may be easier for you to open up your family to other half-sibling families rather than the donor. Therapist Susan Frankel adds that finding half siblings can also be "more direct and uncomplicated by so much adult overlay and concerns."

For children with anonymous donors, finding half siblings is more realistic than finding the donor. At around age nine, Ryan understood that he would probably never get to meet his anonymous donor, but he realized (with some relief) that there were others out there from the same donor—others with whom he might share similar traits. The prospect of connecting with these children was very exciting; it inspired Ryan and Wendy to start the DSR, which now serves as the primary resource for families who want to connect with half siblings and willing donors.

My Child Never Asks Any Questions. How Do I Start a Discussion?

While many parents wish for easier questions, some parents wish their children asked any questions at all. Terry, a single mother, waited until her daughter's tenth birthday to tell her that she had been donor-conceived. Although Terry was curious about the donor and wanted to meet half siblings, her daughter was not. Even after Terry found out about a half-sibling family that lived nearby, her daughter showed no interest. Terry was surprised that her daughter didn't want to know anything about her donor family, and she was a little worried that her daughter was not dealing with her feelings about being donor-conceived.

Like Terry, you might find that your child shows no interest in finding out more about the donor or potential half siblings or anything else related to her donor conception. Just as in the world of adoption, some children have a burning desire to know more about their biological family members, some are mildly curious, and some have no interest at all. Take this as an expression of their personality, and perhaps a reflection of their age and current maturity level, not an example of denial.

If, instead, you think your child may have questions and concerns that she is not comfortable expressing, then create opportunities that allow her to explore any feelings she might have. Continue to weave the donor into family discussions, both to make sure your child knows you are comfortable discussing the donor and to make sure she is digesting this fact of her life instead of repressing it. You can, for example, discuss family resemblances. In two-parent families, discuss what mannerisms or facial expressions have been picked up from both parents, the biological and the nonbiological parent. What attributes most likely come from the donor? Where did their sense of humor come from? Or their amazing sense of balance? (Be careful not to ascribe all negative characteristics to the donor.)

The more openly and honestly you can look at both the similarities and the differences between you and your child, the more comfortable it will be for everyone. Talking about how all of us are a unique combination of both nature and nurture lets your child begin to understand that who he is is a result of many contributing factors: the parents who raise him, the community, the donor, and the genetic heritage of both biological parents.

Family Dynamics

As you focus on your relationship with your child, don't forget about the rest of the family. If you have a partner-parent, then pay attention to your relationship. Make sure to stay on the same page, supporting each other and, most important, your child as dialogue unfolds and questions are raised. If you and your co-parent are no longer together, try to cooperate and reinforce the same message. Children should not see conflict between their parents.

As you focus on your child's reaction, you must also, if you have other children, consider the revelation's impact on them. Siblings who thought they were a full genetic family will need to redefine their relationships, as we saw with Denise. Families can be in a state of flux while everyone digests the information. Most families, though, like Denise's, come to the realization that even though full genetic relatives are now known to be only half siblings, their love and connection to each other doesn't change at all.

If you have more than one child, then each may have entered your family in a different way—without donors, with different donors, with the same donor, or by adoption or marriage. Make sure that each child knows how much he or she is loved. Even if your children are all donor-conceived, they might have different curiosities and desires: where one is curious about his donor and donor half siblings, another may never want to discuss having been donor-conceived at all.

"My mother told my sister and me that we were donor-conceived when we were twenty-one (me) and twenty-four (my sister). My parents divorced when I was two years old and my dad was living upstate. It was quite an awkward and stilted conversation and my mom went for a long drive afterward. I think she was shaking. Right after she told me, I laughed in disbelief. It was a huge shock. Don't underestimate the amount of time your kids might need to process the information. I think it took me two or three years. I think the older the children are, the more their identity has already been formed, and the more difficult the rearrangement can be.

"If I can give you some reassurances, our family life continued pretty much as normal. I didn't feel anger toward my mother because I understood that secrecy was the norm of the era and she was told not to tell us. She never had any support and no one ever gave her any advice on how to tell.

"I could also tell that it was tremendously difficult for her to do it, because by nature she is not a confrontational person, so I respected her bravery and honesty.

"My sister and I swung separate ways. It became extremely important for me to find the identity of our donor, while my sister tried to minimize what had happened, and put it behind her, and not dwell on it. I've asked my mother lots of questions, and she's given me a copy of the donor profile, which she had kept in her bank safety deposit box. That really helps, even though she doesn't know anything else about him."

Address each child's needs individually, responding, as always, with honesty, confidence, and sensitivity to your child's experience of the situation. Listen to what your child tells you she wants. Talk to each child separately so they don't feel pressure from their siblings. Siblings will vary in their curiosity, and one may want to meet the donor tomorrow while another may be unable to understand why anyone would ever want to meet members of their donor family. You should reassure them that you respect their privacy, making sure they understand you will not share information behind their backs with other children or with family members. On the other hand, remind them that you are a family and make sure they appreciate their siblings' differing attitudes, including interest in reaching out to other genetic family members. As Wendy has repeatedly seen during her consults, families can successfully maneuver the differing levels of curiosity among their children through honesty and clarity.

Be direct in responding to your children. Remind them that nothing has changed. Talk to them about how their bonds with family members are created by both biology and affection (for example, they may adore your brother's spouse, with whom there is no biological relationship whatsoever).

Once everyone in the nuclear family is reasonably comfortable, extended family members can be brought into the conversation. Many parents share their infertility struggles with those close to them, in which case others will have known for years by the time an older child is told. But in families where a child is told when she is younger, parents and child can decide together whom to tell and when to do it; while toddlers may not be at all concerned about this, your school-age child can have strong preferences, and it is important to involve them in deciding what to tell others. Ultimately, your older child is the only one who can say whether she is comfortable sharing this information about her origins.

And even once she is ready, it is important for you both to acknowledge, despite our belief in the urgency of honesty in most situations, that some family members might not be able to react gracefully and supportively to this part of your story. (After all, some people can't even handle hearing the word "sperm.") Spend some time together before you put your revelation out there, imagining the way it might be received, and help your child understand the differing attitudes toward donor conception. You and your child will need to be patient and keep sharing your experiences, thoughts, and feelings with your family, so that they too can come to accept this new information.

Even for family members who have always known, information about half-sibling families or even of a connection with the donor can be big news. Some families choose to talk to one family member at a time. Other families call a family meeting or wait until a regularly scheduled get-together. Assess your own family's dynamics to figure out which approach will work best for you.

Your Own Feelings

After the initial telling, you may still feel unsettled. You'll remember how unpleasant it was to struggle with infertility, how disappointed you felt in giving up on finding a supportive second parent, or how difficult it was to find the right donor (even though you did). For parents of teens, you may joke that your child's donor was actually an "alien" when your child exhibits new and confusing behaviors (you may wonder whether alpha male or queen bee girl behaviors really can be inherited). If your child feels deceived, mistrustful, or angry, you may question her love for you and your worth as a parent.

Don't repress your own emotional reactions in the name of supporting your child. As we emphasized in Chapter 2, you need to confront your unresolved feelings about donor conception. Olivia Montuschi, a counselor who cofounded Britain's Donor Conception Network, points out, "The uncomfortable truth is that very few of us would have chosen to have a child in this way."[1] Acknowledging this truth may allow you to move on to appreciating the fact that you did, and do, have a child after all.

You may be wondering how parenting a donor-conceived child differs from other kinds of parenting, and some days you may not feel up to the challenge. As your child grows, you may be disappointed that he is not turning out the way you expected, or you may notice how much he differs from his cousins or even your children from an earlier marriage. You may be concerned, Ellen Sarasohn Glazer points out, about whether your child has inherited some of your donor's "less appealing traits. You may feel added sadness that some qualities you'd hoped to see in your child seem to be missing."[2]

One of the first pieces of parenting advice given to Naomi, whose children are not donor-conceived, was: Whatever expectations you have for your children, lose them now. Let your children develop their own personalities. Don't ever compare them to the fantasy child lurking in your mind. This advice applies in every family. Olivia Montuschi explains that when her donor-conceived son was seven or eight, she was finally "able to mourn the child we couldn't have together and accept our son for the truly lovely person he really is. I could not feel closer to him now."[3] If you have similar feelings, we hope you have dealt with them long before your child turns seven; otherwise, it can be challenging to remain open and nonjudgmental as you respond to your child.

Some parents who used donors say that they are surprised not to feel constantly joyous about their children, having gone through so much just to have them. Glazer points out that, once they have a baby, parents of donor-conceived children are "grateful—*very grateful*—but they are also tired, stressed, ambivalent and inexperienced," like any other parent. "Many become angry with themselves and remorseful when they feel the normal feelings of new parents—fatigued, trapped and wondering, *what have I gotten myself into?*"[4] Like all parents, you need to learn to have patience with yourself and with your child. This patience will come in handy when your child asks questions that make you uncomfortable.

At some point, as your child continues to ask questions, as you become even more comfortable managing your family's dynamics, your child is likely to start wondering: Can I find other people who I am related to?

chapter six

The Decision to Search

Your work is to discover your world and then
with all your heart give yourself to it.

· BUDDHA ·

I f you are a parent who used an anonymous donor, you have probably become interested, as you've watched your child develop, in discovering her other genetic half—the origin of some of those wonderful qualities whose source is a mystery to you. If your child is young, you may also be curious about the other parents who have chosen your donor, and you might be interested in connecting with those parents yourself, as well as in finding half siblings for your child. Perhaps you've felt regret about the donor-shaped hole in your lives. On the other hand, perhaps the prospect of meeting him or her still unsettles you. Even if you do not want to search for the donor, you might still seek out more information and try to establish communication with others who have used the same eggs or sperm. Finding your child's half siblings can expand your community of support, affection, and kinship.

"For anyone who still doesn't understand why we donor-conceived adults feel such a strong need to find our donors, I heard a quote the other day which was in reference to adoptees but is just as applicable to us. 'We know our families love us and wanted us enough to go to "extraordinary measures" to have us, but who wants to start a book on Chapter 2? I want Chapter 1, the Introduction, and the Prologue as well!'"

—*Nina, age twenty-five*

Like adopted children, donor offspring vary in the intensity of their desire to find biological relatives. While some are scarcely curious, others feel painfully incomplete without contact. If you are a donor-conceived person, you are probably at least a little bit curious about your donor and possible half siblings, whether you are simply interested in learning more information about your ancestry and your medical history or hopeful about establishing relationships with your biological kin.

Moving from curiosity to action and initiating your search can happen whenever you are ready. Would-be parents considering whether to use a particular donor might look for other parents and offspring as part of their research. While typically parents and offspring are the ones who are searching, increasing numbers of donors are also deciding to try to find their offspring. Sometimes, relatives of offspring and donors search too, and they have a variety of reasons: for example, parents of deceased donors may hope to find their genetic grandchildren, or family members may assist a donor child who has lost her only known parent and is seeking connection with her genetic relatives.

Even if you are incredibly excited about the possibility of finding genetic relatives, you might also have some reservations and uncertainties about searching. For parents and offspring, knowing what you want from the search—whether it is a name, a photo, weekly phone calls, or cozy holidays together—will focus and direct your process.

Wendy's Search

Wendy's search was prompted by her child's urgent curiosity about his origins. She had been open with Ryan ever since, as a two-year-old, he started asking about his missing father. But openness was not enough; young as he was, Ryan wanted information, and Wendy didn't even have a simple donor profile. By the time he was three, Ryan's questions about his father had convinced Wendy that they needed to find out more.

The older Ryan became, the more Wendy could see attributes and characteristics that clearly didn't come from her or her side of the family. When Ryan was three, Wendy called her clinic. It had no information about the donor himself but did provide the name of the sperm bank and his donor number. After making some more phone calls, Wendy received the donor profile in the mail. She left the envelope on the kitchen counter for a day before bracing herself to tear it open, excited and nervous. She studied the donor profile: he had been a towhead as a child but now had brown hair. He had brown eyes, high verbal and math SAT scores, and degrees in engineering. His brother was a blond-haired pilot. For the first time, she started to picture the invisible pieces of Ryan's DNA. She finally understood where Ryan got his brown eyes, blond hair, and so much more, such as his facility with language and maybe even why he was so interested in airplanes.

Included with the donor profile was a short, handwritten note, her donor's response to the question: "If we could pass along a message to the recipient(s) of your semen, what would that message be?" Donor 1058 wrote: "Educate the child. Raise him/her without biases of any kind. Teach him/her to trust in others but to rely on self. Instill in him/her a sense of humor and the ability to enjoy life." Wendy's eyes filled with tears. That note profoundly affected her parenting, setting a goal for how she wanted to raise Ryan. It also made Donor 1058 more real to Wendy. He wasn't just a vial of sperm that had given her the ability to have a child, but a kind and thoughtful person whom she was relieved to know had given his genes to her son. Back in 1993, however, that was it: no more information was available beyond the nonidentifying donor profile. This was long before daily usage of the Internet, widespread availability of DNA testing, and the creation of the DSR, which make searching much easier today.

Preparing to Search: Parents

Researchers from Cambridge University and the DSR have worked together to achieve a better understanding of the most common motivations for searching:

- To connect with other parents who have used the same donor
- To support my child
- To satisfy my curiosity about similarities in appearance and personalities
- To connect with the donor
- To share and update medical information with the donor and/ or half siblings
- To collect information about ancestry and genetic background
- To create a larger kin network
- To thank the donor

These compelling reasons to search must often be weighed against uncertainty, fear, partners' preferences, and incomplete understandings of parental legal rights as people consider whether to start the process. Many people feel a need to clear their plates before they begin to search, to make sure that they have adequate time and emotional energy. On the other hand, searching can often be exhilarating, even for people who are dealing with the usual stress of busy lives at work and at home. It opens up new possibilities for their children and themselves. Be prepared to have multiple, potentially ambivalent feelings about the different levels of connecting. DSR mom Isabel said that she wanted to "understand more about those who may be biologically related to my children. I'm not sure if I'm ready to meet anyone, but perhaps we can exchange information that would be helpful to one another."

If you don't feel quite ready yet, carefully consider what is coming between you and beginning the search. You might have convinced yourself that you must first complete other business, such as finishing a bathroom remodel or getting promoted at work, so that you can truly focus your energy. Or you may have emotional barriers that prevent you from moving forward, like the need to resolve different approaches with your partner. Recognize what is really stopping you, so that you don't put off the search indefinitely: Will you really be ready once you have a new bathtub, or is something else going on? When you stop to think rationally about why you don't feel ready, you may realize how strongly your emotions are controlling your actions.

Ensure that your emotions are fully engaged in moving forward to help give you perspective on your next step. Instead of, for example, focusing on the difficulties of negotiating this issue with your partner (of course, you will still need to deal with this), focus instead on the significant emotional reward that connecting can bring for you and, more importantly, for your child. Imagine how a half-sibling connection might enrich their lives. Meeting others who share characteristics, interests, and physical attributes might be life changing, especially for those who have grown up having been "only" children.

Preparing to Search:
Donor-Conceived People

"My name is Harry and I found out I was a donor offspring when I was seventeen years old, before I left for college. I was immediately curious as to who my donor was, what he looked like, was he a nice man, and whether or not I had other 'siblings' that I don't know about. My mother told me that both my sister and I were created through different sperm donors, and things finally made sense. I have black hair and brown eyes, and my sister has red hair, green eyes, pale skin, and freckles. Now that I am twenty-one years old, I have a strong urge to find my donor father. I would love to just see a picture of him to see if there are similarities. I look a lot like my mother, but I have always wondered what was on the other side."

Even if you are extremely curious about your donor family, starting your search may take a few years, as you ponder all the possible scenarios that might result from your search. There's no rush, and there's no one time when "everyone" is ready. Searching *does* let you transform your questions about your past into concrete actions. The 2010 movie *The Kids Are All Right* focused popular culture's attention on why offspring search, the differing levels of interest in each family, and what happens when they find their donors. Laser and Joni are half siblings conceived using the same donor; their mothers, played by Annette Bening and Julianne Moore, are married to each other. Laser, like many donor offspring cresting adolescence, becomes extremely curious about their donor and begs his older sister to help him search for him. Although Joni is worried about hurting her mothers and doesn't seem as curious as Laser, she agrees to his plan. It turns out to be surprisingly easy to find Paul, the donor: Joni simply calls the sperm bank. Meeting the donor does not ultimately expand their kinship network, but Laser and Joni learn a lot that is both painful and joyous about themselves and their family. Although this Hollywood representation of the ease with which offspring can locate their donors is misleading, it does illustrate some of the motivations for searching and a few of the complex situations (both probable and highly unlikely) that might result from finding the donor. As you prepare to search, Laser and Joni's experiences—along with the other stories of donor-conceived people in this book—can help you appreciate the need to be prepared for whatever you will find.

Searching to Learn More about Yourself and to Find a Community

The Cambridge/DSR study of the experiences of donor offspring as they sought and contacted their half siblings and donors found that almost everyone searched for their half siblings because they were curious about similarities in appearance and personality.[1] But the study found many other reasons people search for their donor and half siblings:

- To see what he/she looks like
- To learn about their ancestry
- To learn more about themselves
- To learn about their medical background
- To tell them who they were
- To establish a relationship

In addition to looking for similarities with others, offspring were particularly interested in being able "to know and understand a 'missing' part of me." The study also concluded that offspring from single-mother families were more likely than those from other family types to search in order to find a new family member. Wendy has also found this to be true on the DSR—offspring from single-mother families without siblings or dads at home do seem to be more active in their search for half siblings and donors. Because their own nuclear families are small, they can be particularly excited about expanding their kinship communities. This was certainly true for Gavin Shuler, whose SMC, Cheryl, wrote in her book, *Sperm Donor = Dad*, about her son's long-held hope for a big family. He wanted a big family with brothers and sisters and cousins,[2] and this led to his finding many new half siblings and his donor on the DSR.

When offspring search for *donors*, almost nine out of ten cite curiosity about the characteristics of the donor as a reason. They are also very interested in getting "a better understanding of 'why I am who I am' and 'in learning about their background.'" For many people, the search for the donor is a search to learn more about themselves. As Sean explained, "Because my interests, appearance, life views, and personality are quite different from my parents', I frequently become curious about which traits I inherited from my biological father." You may be hoping to resolve questions you have about where you belong. In fact, donor offspring commonly report surprise, relief, and even a sense of peace when they find relatives with similar mannerisms, physical attributes, temperaments, and interests. As Katrina, a donor-conceived college student, explained, when her biological father first e-mailed her with his picture, "From my computer screen, my own face seemed to stare back at me. And just like that, after seventeen years, the missing piece of the puzzle snapped into place. The puzzle of who I am."[3]

Searching to Learn More about Your Health

Many people search to discover their medical histories, to learn about their donor's health as well as any conditions experienced by half siblings. They want to plan for any potential health issues, getting the proper screenings and relevant preventive care. They may want to see if half siblings have developed similar medical conditions. So even if you have no interest in meeting the donor or half siblings, filling in these missing medical blanks can be crucial for making decisions on health care screenings and checkups and for maintaining your health.

Parents often look through hundreds of donor profiles before finding the "perfect" donor, such as someone they believe is a healthy six-foot, two-inch medical student with blue eyes and a passion for music. What they don't know, however, is if he has a genetic defect that will manifest itself years after he made his donation; they won't know if he subsequently drops out of medical school and becomes a drug addict. They also won't know if the donor already has fifty children out there, with a high percentage of the parents reporting that their children are on the autism spectrum. There are no legal limits on the number of children who can be conceived through one donor's gametes, and there is no legally required tracking, updating, and sharing of medical records. Unlike the world of adoption, which has numerous laws focused on the best interest of the child, there is little regulation of donor conception. The minimal regulation that does exist concerns the interests of would-be parents solely as patients and consumers; the fertility industry is a business, not an enterprise focused on the best interests of children.

Donor profiles typically provide relatively little health information. The profile is a snapshot of one day in the life of a healthy young donor. Until 2005, no federal law even required donors to be screened for sexually transmitted diseases. There is still no federal law requiring that donors be screened for various genetically transmitted diseases, such as Tay-Sachs. The only ways to find out more about a specific donor are to perform DNA testing on the sperm or to connect with others who have used the same donor to find out their experiences. In fact, the DSR lists many inherited illnesses such as cystic fibrosis, hemochromatosis, and even fatal genetic heart conditions that could be prevented with more comprehensive screening; checking out the DSR before an insemination can protect your child against otherwise unknown medical and genetic issues. (As you'll see in Chapter 12, this isn't the way it has to be; new state and national laws could set limits on the numbers of donor offspring/donors and could require additional testing.)

Sperm banks ship to many small clinics around the world. There is no system for maintaining proper records of live births and how those babies develop. You may have dozens of half siblings in Mexico, Brazil, Denmark, or many other countries. Two of the largest US sperm banks brag that they ship sperm to between fifty and sixty countries around the world. Some of the smaller clinics that import this sperm don't tell recipient families where the sperm originated, and some even renumber the donors so there is simply no way to share medical records and information among parents or even through the sperm bank and donors.

Once they donate, donors are rarely contacted for medical updates. Nevertheless, donors often feel that they or their close family members do have medical or genetic issues that should be shared with families. These conscientious donors can inform their banks or agencies about their concerns but have no way of ensuring that the information is transmitted to the families who need it. In fact, Wendy has heard from numerous donors and parents who have repeatedly called their sperm banks to report updated health information, but they have never even received a return call. Some banks have reportedly taken the medical information, but when other families have called in, those families are told, "No medical updates are on file."

As long as the majority of banks and agencies fail to act as clearing-houses for vital medical information, the only way to find it is to find the donor. Finding half siblings can also help complete a medical profile, although in a more ambiguous way. Families can, and do, share and update this type of medical information on the DSR every day. Some do so while establishing strong familial connections, while others share medical information anonymously.

Ultimately, you need to learn as much medical information about yourself as possible. The sooner you know about familial medical issues, the sooner you'll be able to make more educated choices about your own health care. The U.S. Surgeon General points out that "family health history is such a powerful screening tool" and strongly encourages all Americans to find out more about this history.[4] Gathering new medical information is extremely helpful, even if it can also be stressful: no one is thrilled to uncover genetic diseases or psychological issues that may be hereditary. You should also share your own medical information with your genetic relatives. For example, if you have been diagnosed with diabetes or have had a positive skin cancer screening, you can encourage your half siblings, donors, or offspring to participate in more thorough or regular blood or dermatology screenings. You can help them become more aware of warning signs that they might not otherwise be focused on.

Rebecca discovered, almost by accident, that her donor had a life-threatening medical issue. She was then able to alert several of her son's half siblings, some of whom ended up testing positive for the genetic heart disorder:

I FOUND MY SON'S DONOR *in 2008 and discovered that he suffered an aortic dissection in 2007 and nearly died. It turned out to be a genetic defect in the connective tissue of the aortic root. His two brothers and his mother also had the same problem. When my son was checked, he also had the same heart defect. His open-heart surgery to correct the problem was in June of 2010. Thanks to the DSR, I was also able to alert the parents of the five known half sibs. I was also able to find the two other clinics where the donor donated and alert them.*

Searching to Satisfy Other Curiosities about Your Donor

You may want to know much more about your donor. All of those questions (for instance: Does my donor think about me? Why did she help create me?) can lead you toward searching. Many donor-conceived people simply want to give the donor the opportunity to know that they exist.

Timmy, a ten-year-old, explained his goals:

> **I WOULD ASK THE DONOR** *to please come forward. I myself would just like to know a little bit about you or see a picture of you. I understand that you have your own family and life and it wouldn't be a problem if you wanted to not have a relationship as father and son but just to be able to talk to you and find out things about myself that my moms can't tell me about 'cause only you would know the answers to. I would also like to see a picture of you so I can see whether we resemble each other. If that is all you would be willing to give, I would be happy with just that. If you would want to know more about me, that would be even better, but I understand that you did this anonymously, but maybe as you get older you might have a change of heart and would want to know about all of us that are out here. I know that I want to know about my donor dad.*

Timmy's hope—that his donor, who signed up for anonymity, may have a change of heart—is actually quite realistic. As their own life circumstances change, some donors still wish to retain their anonymity, but many others become interested in connecting with the children that they helped to create. He accurately describes the curiosity of so many donor-conceived people, as well as their desire for their donors to be curious about them. And like most offspring, he shows great respect for the donor's current family and life; his goal is to respond to the donor's situation, not pursue connection regardless of the donor's preferences.

Questions and Hesitations about Searching and Connecting

Not everyone decides to search for relatives, although most people do think about it at some point. Searching is not a mandatory requirement of being part of a donor family or the greater donor community. Take the time to explore your feelings, hesitations, concerns, and desires.

WHAT WE FEAR WHEN WE THINK ABOUT SEARCHING

- We don't know who and what we might find: How will unknown relatives measure up to any expectations we have about them?

- We might find "too many" genetic relatives.

- Our expectations might be vastly different from those of the people we find.

(continued)

- ☀ Our new connections might interfere with our family and life.

- ☀ We might learn troubling news about potential medical issues.

- ☀ What if our search is unsuccessful?

"It's Unnecessary"

Some parents believe their children do not need the additional information and connections that might result from searching. And indeed, some donor-conceived people feel as though their identities and lives are 100 percent complete and therefore have no urge to track down genetic relatives. Richard explained: "I never once felt disconnected from the people who raised me. They are my parents in every sense of the word. That is where I come from and I don't challenge it, question it, or feel any sense of loss over not knowing a biological donor."

Searching for a donor or half siblings might be entirely superfluous for people like Richard, who seem to be confident in their identities, content in their family membership, and uninterested in any further information. This is entirely their decision: they have the tools if they ever do become interested. They should remain open to the possibility that their curiosities and desires may change over time. Curiosity has a way of ebbing and flowing over the course of a donor-conceived person's life.

"We Are a Family Like Any Other, and We Want to Keep It That Way"

Some parents prefer to concentrate on the family they have built rather than declare their difference by reaching out into the unknown. Connecting to other families formed through donor conception may remind them that they were not able to get pregnant the traditional way. For heterosexual couples, their family now looks like any other; they have formed what Vassar professor Molly Shanley calls the "as if" family, the family that would have been formed without infertility. They may prefer not to celebrate or even acknowledge their own special circumstances as they try to blend in. Tamsin Eva, a librarian and writer who is the mother of toddlers born through donor conception, explained her reluctance to search in the *New York Times* in the summer of 2012.[5] Although she had signed up for the Donor Sibling Registry, like many others who sign up, she was passively "lurking," not posting: "I simply didn't know if I was ready to acknowledge the connection. I had also wanted to feel ordinary for a little while longer."

Searching can feel like opening Pandora's box if parents have conflicting emotions about searching for the donor. There might be a lot of anxiety about making contact with people who are complete strangers, yet, at the same time, close biological relatives to your children. You might not want to be reminded of your partner's (or your own) lack of genetic connection. Why mess with what is currently a great parent-child relationship?

Even families that don't "look" traditional may strive to maintain a certain ordinariness. For single women, entry into a donor community might provide connections with other single mothers, but it is also a marker of difference, of going beyond their existing social networks. For LGBTQ families, donor conception may be so casually accepted that reaching out to others seems unnecessary. Rather than initiating a search process that will be unfamiliar to most of their peers, donor-conceived people in any kind of family may want to live as though their origins have not really affected them.

"I Don't Want to Share My Donor"

Some people, on the other hand, want to believe that their unique child doesn't share DNA with any half siblings. These parents think of the donor as belonging to them alone, and, according to sociologist Rosanna Hertz, they have difficulty accepting that other children have also been created by their special donor—maybe even five, ten, or seventy-five others.[6] Some women have even reported that they feel a strange sense of "infidelity" because their donor helped to create other children. Wendy has even met mothers who have purposely bought up all remaining vials for their donor, trying to prohibit others from having children from *their* donor.

It can be hard to accept that your child has half siblings unknown to you, that they share DNA, and that your donor did, in fact, contribute eggs or sperm to other families. Of course, you understand that your donor sold gametes. That's how you selected the donor in the first place, and if your donor had qualities that were desirable to you, it's only reasonable to suppose that others found those qualities desirable as well. Your understanding the situation doesn't necessarily mean that you want to think about those other families.

Let's banish this uneasiness by acknowledging that your child—that every child—is unique. The donor only contributed half of your child's genetic makeup, and you are the ones nurturing your child. If you (and your partner) had conceived two children without using a donor, you would not worry that they were insufficiently distinguished as individuals because they shared the same DNA. In fact, finding other members of your donor family can help you appreciate just how distinctive your child actually is, as you compare and contrast characteristics of half siblings. If your child wants to find genetic relatives, that desire should trump your misgivings. The very thing that you are afraid of—finding others with the same donor—could be incredibly comforting to your child, who will revel in the ways he resembles the people with whom he shares that invisible side of himself.

Hearing stories about large groups of siblings can also be unsettling. If incorporating one or two new family members into your life seems daunting, the possibility of encountering twenty, fifty, one hundred, or even more is probably downright frightening. But this concern should not hold you back from searching. Many families have successfully connected with dozens of others on the DSR; their stories show that you can manage such large connections, too.

"It's Better Not to Know"

The uncertain outcome of searching can make it seem very scary, not just for parents but also for donors and donor-conceived people. Anyone who searches cannot say in advance who and what they might find, how many genetic relatives are actually out there, and whether these new connections will interfere with their family and their life.

Donor-conceived people might have some fear and anxiety about being rejected by donors or half siblings. Or, if you hope to find supplementary information rather than a relationship, perhaps you worry that making contact will require you to enter a situation that you are just not ready for. Expectations differ wildly, as does the speed with which people acclimate to newfound relationships. Having fantasized about your donor as a superhero or Nobel Prize winner, you might be scared about what will happen when you come face-to-face with a perfectly imperfect human being. And what about incorporating new biological relatives into the existing family? Will everyone get along? Will your parents feel hurt or angry? What will Grandma think?

Parents can also have nightmares about an unknown donor making legal claims on the child. This is an entirely unrealistic fear. Particularly for LGBTQ parents, however, who may have faced discrimination in their quest to start a family in the first place, this can be a strong fear while their children are young. In the thousands of donor families Wendy knows through the DSR, and in all the cases we have read about, unknown donors have never been known to assert legal rights. We have never heard of an unknown donor tracking down a child and claiming to be the legal parent. The few highly publicized cases involving donors claiming rights or being forced to pay child support involve known donors who haven't followed state laws that would terminate their rights.[7]

The donors with whom Wendy has talked over the years have all been very respectful of the fact that the children they've helped to create already have "parents." Just as the offspring searching are not looking for a "dad" or a "mom," most donors are not looking to be "parents." They want to offer information, learn more about their donor offspring, and carefully explore what types of relationships the parents and children might be open to having.

You may feel that it is better not to learn about families who will want a different level of contact than you are prepared for, whether that's more or less than what you're looking for. What if they are not ready to jump on a plane the next day to come and meet you? What if you are not ready to jump on that plane? What if they are only willing to share medical information? What if you connect with a mother who hasn't told her children that they are donor-conceived?

Expectations and the speed with which we move through this new territory can certainly vary. Remember that this is your search process, and you are in control over whether, and when, you decide to jump on that plane. While you should be aware of the possibilities of dead ends and differing interests, don't let them paralyze you if you really are interested in finding members of your donor family.

"No One Around Me Thinks This Is a Good Idea"

People in your own family or in your community may discourage your interest in searching. They might tell you, *"Those* people are unimportant" or *"They* are not your real family." Family members might give ultimatums, "It's us or them!" They may even try to frame searching as a betrayal or an act of disloyalty to them. This can confuse and upset both parents and offspring, or even convince them that they should stifle their natural curiosity rather than hurt others. In situations like this, consider family counseling. Make sure that you and your children know that this is the other person's issue, not yours, and remind yourselves that you have every right to make choices about discovering and connecting with new family members. Social worker Kris Probasco suggests that you maintain boundaries that protect your decision making so that other family members understand they cannot interfere. When it comes to others, communicate with them and hope that they will put aside their own insecurities and fears in order to support you. Don't let their anxieties stop you; stay focused on what you want and follow your own heart.

Sadly, some parents, older offspring, and even donors end up searching without support from family members, and so they need to search surreptitiously. This can create even more challenging situations when donors or half siblings are found and you feel that you can't share your discoveries and excitement. Try to find ways to introduce the information in a nonthreatening manner so that you create an opportunity for your hesitant relatives to gradually absorb what you are experiencing and feeling. Whatever reassurances or time they might need is worth it for your ongoing relationship with them. You may win your family's support yet if they have time to think through the situation, balancing the benefits of a successful search against their own phantom fears.

How to Resolve Uncertainties

Now that you've read through other people's reasons for searching and not searching, make your own list of pros and cons. You might make a formal written list, or you might be processing these hesitations less formally. Whatever you do, try to be as precise as possible about your hopes and hesitations, and let yourself be open and nonjudgmental. For instance, if you make a formal list, then you might write, "I want to be able to answer my child's questions," and then review any specific questions your child has asked that you hope to answer. If you think to yourself, "I don't want to find so many half siblings that I don't know what to do," really imagine the scenario, how it might make you feel, and then figure out ways you might negotiate it.

As you go through this process, you are likely to discover that your fears are more manageable than you anticipated. If not, then ask for help as you work through your doubts and fears. You can talk to your parents, friends, colleagues, and others about your decision making, as well as a counselor, and you can read about others' experiences on the DSR. There are many "Success Stories" posted there by people who once had hesitations about making contact. Whether you decide to search or not, this is your decision, and you should feel comfortable with it.

For some personalities, decisions bubble up from the back of the brain without formal lists and pre-imagined scenarios. Essayist Tamsin Eva, who didn't want to feel different, took the first step toward connection only after reading a book about donor conception to her four-year-old child. Overcoming her fear of leaving behind her "old normal," she then typed her first post on the DSR Web site. Less than a week later, after she connected with several other mothers who had used the same donor and with whom she felt very comfortable, they created their own Facebook group. She has embraced her "new normal," and she's happy that her children will grow up with those whom she calls "diblings," their genetically related half siblings.

Managing Expectations for Your Search

Some people want an occasional exchange of basic medical and genetic history; some people simply want to know how many half siblings exist; others dream of visiting Disney World together. A clear idea at the start will help you focus your search, establish reasonable expectations, and communicate clearly right away with newfound donor family members. Of course, recognize that your goals may change over time.

WHAT DO YOU WANT FROM YOUR SEARCH?

- Do you wish to remain anonymous?

- Do you want a simple exchange of information? Do you want to exchange photos, medical information, and e-mails on the DSR?

- What questions do you want to ask your donor and/or half siblings?

- What information are you willing to share? Medical? Psychological? Other?

(continued)

- ☀ Do you want to meet your donor and/or half siblings and their parents?

- ☀ Do you want to establish a long-term relationship?

- ☀ Do you want your donor and/or half siblings to establish relationships with your whole family?

- ☀ Do you want a Facebook friendship?

Reading other people's stories about searching and finding can help you establish realistic goals, which are the best preparation for contact. You'll find many such stories in later chapters and also on the DSR. They should enhance your confidence about how meaningful it can be to connect with previously unknown genetic relatives and establish new relationships with them.

As you establish goals, you should also mentally prepare for less than optimal outcomes. For instance, you may have to wait months, years, or even forever to find a genetic relative. Ryan, who was the first to post on the DSR, waited *seven years* before his half sister joined, making them the 2,910th and 2,911th people to match on the DSR. His half sister, on the other hand, found Ryan and sent him a message on the DSR within *minutes* of joining.

Another potential result is a successful search that doesn't turn up exactly what you had hoped to find. The 2010 documentary *Donor Unknown* featured donor Jeffrey, a free-spirited, eccentric nomad living in a camper in Venice Beach, California. While many of his offspring had established wonderful connections among themselves, they still longed to know about their genetic father. Finding him, however, proved to be quite a surprise. What they read about on the donor profile didn't precisely match up with the reality they found. Some things did match up, however, such as his love for animals and his blue eyes (although they had not realized that he was a former *Playgirl* centerfold model).

Try not to build unrealistic expectations about your donor or half siblings. Some of your expectations may be met, and even exceeded, but you also need to be ready for some possible disappointments. Be prepared, as you undertake the search, to call on your support system: family members, friends, and others in the donor community who have lived through these situations. Remember to focus on the positive. Every day of your life holds the possibility of a new family member making contact with you.

PREPARING YOURSELF

1. Be willing to honor the boundaries established by your new genetic relatives.

2. Acknowledge that your donor or half siblings may come from different religious backgrounds, or may have different sexual orientations or different socio-economic or political backgrounds.

3. Understand that your donor may turn out to be entirely different from the image you've developed—not the Nobel winner he claimed to be.

4. Consider that your egg donor may have been diagnosed with breast cancer, or that your sperm donor

(continued)

> may have only recently learned that he is a carrier for a genetic disease.
>
> 5. Recognize that your donor may get cold feet and close the door before you've had a chance to talk.
>
> 6. Remember that you may not feel an immediate closeness with your half siblings and/or donor.

Knowing When to Search

There is no magical age at which all children, or their parents, are ready to search or connect. Most people begin to search shortly after deciding to do so, but some people wait. For instance, families whose donor indicated that they would be willing to be known when the child reaches eighteen may wait until then, perhaps searching only for half siblings in the meantime. Or they may be able to overcome their own fears. Every family must consider its own circumstances.

Some people wonder whether it makes sense to search early in order to give their child the opportunity to connect when he or she is young, or whether they should wait until the child is old enough to decide for himself. We are glad to see many parents start searching when their children are born (or even before conception). Some parents on the DSR say that they feel regret for not having initiated the search process earlier; the longer you wait, the more difficult it can become, both practically and emotionally. Thousands of families with young children integrate half siblings and donors into their families successfully and joyfully. Many donor-conceived people have shared that they are happy they began to search as early as they could. Naomi's husband, Tony, is adopted; he decided to search for his birth parents as an adult. By the time Tony found information about Dorothy, his birth mother, she had died of a brain tumor. Although he was later able to establish a warm and loving relationship with Dorothy's mother, he urges, "Search before it is too late. You don't get a second chance."

Searching: Before and during Pregnancy

> "My partner and I have narrowed our search down to two donors. We have found four sibling families on three continents on the DSR for one of the donors, and two families are posted for the other. We are taking it slow, but plan to e-mail the families to see if their children are healthy and if they might perhaps share photos with us. Whichever donor we decide to use, we are hoping that these families might be a source of support to us in the future."
>
> —*Kayla, potential mother*

As they choose among donors, many people want more information than the sperm banks or egg agencies can provide; they may want to see if medical issues have surfaced or to know how many children might have already been born from the donor. They may want to see photos of children born from the donor and to consider the other parents' compatibility.

It is not at all unusual for women to come to the DSR to connect with half-sibling families, and sometimes donors, before they even get pregnant. Many have established strong kinship bonds with others who are pregnant or who already have children from the same donor. (One couple had connected with their donor on the DSR while they were pregnant, but then, to their great disappointment, had a miscarriage. The donor expressed his sympathy and even sent a condolence card.) Connecting with half-sibling families and sharing medical information, photos, and other information about pregnancies and children can be comforting at this early stage. Single mothers are often excited to find other single mothers who are happy to welcome new additions into their half-sibling family group. It's essentially choosing a donor based on the donor family he has unwittingly created. Searching at this early point can provide you and your child with security and community from the very beginning of your life as a family.

Here is Lucy's story:

> **I HAVE BEEN BLESSED** *to have actually found my donor through the DSR while I was pregnant. We have been in contact over the past year (my daughter is thirteen months old) just a few times. We are both very conscientious and I feel like I couldn't have picked a better donor or situation for my daughter. I feel so lucky to know who he is and to be able to reach him if there are medical concerns. When I was choosing a donor, I had sleepless nights worrying that my donor could die before my daughter reached eighteen or that after eighteen years he may have changed his mind about being willing to be known and dodge my daughter if she chose to seek him out.*

Searching: Parents with Younger Children

While her daughter was a toddler, Harper decided it was important to find her donor. A forty-year-old architect who comes from a close-knit family, Harper didn't want her daughter to grow up without the opportunity to see what her biological father looked like and to ask him questions. Harper also wanted to make sure that her daughter understood her donor conception origins: "I hope that because my daughter will not know anything different than knowing who he is and what his role is in her life, she will not be tormented or go through the difficult processing that I would suspect young children or even young adults might go through when learning who their donors are."

Another mother, Lauren, decided to expand her son's understanding of family while he was young, and she also wanted to find a new community for herself. "If I had not joined the DSR, I would never have gotten to know such wonderful people who are now part of my family. Our children, so far all under the age of five, will grow up knowing each other as brothers and sisters. This will be their normal. I think their lives will definitely be richer for knowing each other. I know mine is."

Ryan was ten when he worked with Wendy to start the DSR. Wendy felt confident that Ryan had been ready for a long time to handle finding his half siblings and donor, but there had been no way to search before then. They entered the very first DSR post together:

> **I AM THE MOTHER** *of an awesome ten-year-old donor child. I know that he has at least three donor siblings and would love to contact them. We are looking for Donor #1058 from the California Cryobank. I hope that this board will serve others looking for their children's (or their own) siblings.*

Their donor had signed up for anonymity, but Ryan wondered if he had since changed his mind. They had no way of knowing if the donor had decided to open himself to contact with offspring. If you and your child are searching together, you should discuss it freely and as often as your child wants to do so, focusing on the possibilities of future connections. Ryan understood that he had the full support and guidance of his mother, and Wendy was careful to frame their search positively.

Some parents don't search while their child is young because they think that eighteen is the magic age to start the process. This could be because some sperm banks offer the option of facilitating contact only when the donor-conceived person reaches that age, and parents thought that searching before their children turned eighteen was a violation of their agreement with the sperm bank. They might even think it would be illegal to search before then. Others signed an agreement with a sperm bank in which they agreed that the bank would protect donor anonymity. Regardless of this agreement, you can certainly look for mutual-consent contact with the donor (even while the bank continues to protect the donor's anonymity). And, of course, your child, who never signed anything, is always free to search.

That's how Riley explained her decision not to search for her donor—and her regrets:

> **PLEASE KNOW,** *I too never wanted to contact the donor before my son was eighteen for several reasons. I didn't want to break my promise/word with the sperm bank, because I agreed that the bank would never reveal my identity to the donor, nor his identity to me. I also didn't want to scare away any men out there who may have wanted to donate, but changed his mind because of having heard about women contacting donors. Had I known then what I know now, I would have searched for him when my son was younger, just to know who he was and have a connection in case, at age eighteen, my son wanted to meet him and he was then unfindable. Please take it from one who has been there: make the connection. You do not have to meet the donor, just make the connection.*

While hindsight is always 20/20, Riley's advice shows that, if you think you will want to connect, search early to increase your chances of connecting. Putting off a search can decrease the chances of locating and making contact with your donor.

Searching: Parents and Adult Children

Many donor-conceived people decide to search during times of transition or after a significant change in personal circumstances. Research shows that some of these milestones are described as:

- "becoming a teenager,"
- "becoming an adult,"
- "getting married or forming a long-term relationship,"
- having "a personal crisis,"
- contracting "an illness or other medical condition," or
- "planning to have children or having children."[8]

Undertaking a search at this point can be both affirming and grounding for you, helping you manage these life events even more confidently. Trust yourself to know when you are ready to embark on your search. While most offspring over the age of eighteen are searching on their own, it's helpful when their parents support their endeavors. If your child is searching, reassure her that you think this is healthy by, for example, consistently expressing interest in the progress of the search. Make sure your child knows that you are open to, and even excited about, her connecting with her half siblings and donor.

Searching: Older Adult Donor Offspring

Most people conceived with donated sperm thirty, forty, fifty, and even more than seventy years ago grew up unaware of their origins, but some were eventually told or found out accidentally. Once they found out, they may not have even thought about the possibility of searching, and they may not have believed they had the right to do so. As they have seen others undertake successful searches, they have realized that they too might be able to find genetic relatives. For them, however, the search process is very difficult. Records are long gone and, for many, their donors are no longer alive. As they develop their expectations about searching, they are likely to focus on half siblings, but most of their half siblings probably never learned the truth about their conception. Surprisingly, the search for the donor may be easier than they anticipated: many of the "donors" during that time period were actually the doctors themselves. (Beginning in the 1940s, Dr. Bertold Wiesner may have "fathered" more than six hundred children through his fertility clinic.)[9] Even when the children and relatives of these doctors are contacted, they are usually not willing to discuss anything with, much less reveal any information to donor-conceived people. While usually shocked to find out that their father or husband "donated" to his patients, children and wives of deceased doctors often seek to protect the memory and integrity of their father/ husband's life and professional legacy by refusing to acknowledge his status as a donor or by refusing any and all contact. The shroud of secrecy that was pervasive back then is tightly maintained.

Consider the advice of Aaron and Sophia, who were conceived in the 1940s when donor conception was shrouded in secrecy, long before sperm banks came into being. Both found out much later in life that they were donor-conceived.

"I AM INTERESTED IN KNOWING *if I have any donor siblings who are still living. Every year, I have less hope that I'll be able to find them since I was conceived back in 1941. But there's always a chance.*"

—*Aaron*

"I WAS BORN IN 1944. *I don't have a donor. I do have a biological father, or at least I used to have one, but he is probably dead by now. I really hope that I can find someone who is closely related to my biological father before I die. That way, I'll be able to know for sure whether he was actually my mother's ob-gyn, because I strongly suspect that's who it was.*"

—*Sophia*

Aaron and Sophia, both approaching seventy, feel quite strongly that they need to search, even though their chances of connecting with their half siblings and certainly with their donors may be slim. Like others, they are ready to move on toward the final aspect of the decision to search: knowing how to search. The next chapter guides you through the search process.

chapter seven

How to Search

In search of my mother's garden,

I found my own.

· ALICE WALKER ·

A quick Internet search brought Ryan's half sister to the Donor Sibling Registry once she decided she was interested in finding her half siblings. She signed up, using only her donor's number and the bank where he had donated. Within seconds, she had matched—with Ryan.

But it's not always that easy. Rich, a sperm donor who decided that he wanted to find his offspring, was frustrated with the sperm bank where he donated for nearly two years. Before he decided to donate, he had thought about the possibility of genetic offspring who might want to contact him. After attending the United States Military Academy at West Point, serving in the army, becoming a big brother, and adopting a seven-year-old boy from state care, he remained curious about children born as a result of his donations. He wrote to the sperm bank, saying he wanted to release it from its promise to protect his confidentiality, but it refused. It would not help him find families who had used his sperm or even disclose his own donor number to him.[1] However, Rich, the winner of the first season of *Survivor*, was a determined man. He discovered the DSR and used it to broadcast his desire to connect. Based on details about his physical appearance and academic background that Rich posted, a man who believed he could be Rich's son contacted him. They both took DNA tests, which confirmed the genetic relationship. As a result, Rich found out his donor number, added it to his posting, and a couple of years later, he also connected with a genetic daughter, again via the DSR.

Looking in All the Right Places

Finding your half-sibling families and donor can be easy, as Ryan's half sister's story shows. If you know your donor number and the name of the facility your parents used, it might be simple to find genetic relatives who have signed up for mutual-consent contact on the DSR, and you may never need to search any further than that.

If you are missing any of this information, or if no one else from your donor cohort has joined the DSR yet, then your search, like Rich's, might not be so simple. In such a situation you'll need to draw on your own reserves of determination and ingenuity and use a variety of resources to locate your genetic relatives or to get basic details about your donor. At this point you might be wondering whether you are now searching for a donor who is not interested in being found. You may worry that your next steps may be an invasion of their privacy. Think long and hard before you proceed with any steps that involve non-mutual-consent contact. Later in the chapter we will discuss the issues surrounding searching for a donor who may not want to be found.

In addition to posting on the Donor Sibling Registry and waiting for mutual-consent contact, you can contact your sperm bank, do DNA testing, and use Internet resources such as Google and Facebook. Combining different strategies provides the most possibilities for finding information. For instance, males can utilize a Y-DNA test. This test might identify some distant male relatives who share a last name, which may also belong to your donor. At the very least, such a name can help direct your search on the Internet, in newspapers, or even in old yearbooks. If out-of-print documents sound far-fetched, consider a case in which you know your donor attended college in your town and played in the university symphony, was an engineering major, or was on the volleyball team. It would not be impossible to track down yearbooks for a number of schools and scan the names and faces for clues.

Some people find it useful to keep a notebook, special computer file, or spreadsheet for notes and leads, as well as a record of actions you've already taken. You don't want to pursue the same false lead twice or constantly interrupt your real search to hunt for stray scraps of paper. Looking back over your notes can also help you develop more leads and determine next steps.

CHECKLIST OF DIFFERENT WAYS TO SEARCH

Search methods depend on whether you are only interested in mutual-consent contact, how much information you already have, the additional types you can collect, and whether you're searching for half siblings and/or your donor.

- ☀ Registering with the DSR
- ☀ Contacting the sperm bank, clinic, or doctor

- ☀ Swabbing your cheek and sending your DNA into a large DNA database

- ☀ Using Internet search engines and social-networking sites

- ☀ Hiring a private investigator

- ☀ Poring through yearbooks, other print resources, and noncomputerized databases

Connecting through the DSR

Posting on the DSR may be all you'll ever need to do to find your genetic relatives. Once you log on to the Web site, even before you yourself have joined and posted, you might see posts from your half siblings or donor— instant match! For those with limited information, more steps might be involved, but many donor offspring have matched on the DSR without knowing their donor numbers. Lisa signed up on the DSR with little information. She had been born in the late 1960s, before commercial sperm banking became big business. The only information she had was the name of her mother's doctor and the city where the doctor practiced, so she was not very optimistic about finding others.

About eight months after Lisa's initial post, a woman e-mailed her to say that her mother had used the same doctor two years later. They teamed up to look for information about their donors, and after a few months of research, they realized that the pool of donors the doctor had used was actually very small. Once they learned about the small donor pool, it occurred to them that they might be half siblings. They took a half-sibling DNA test, and they were amazed that the test came back with virtual certainty that they were sisters. Since then, they've connected with three other half siblings. Lisa's advice: "For all the older donor offspring out there who have only fragments of the story of their conception, don't give up hope."

The DSR has been a successful means of contact for more than ten thousand registrants to date. If you are interested in mutual-consent contact, it's easy to add a posting to the DSR so that you can be found by others who share your donor, or even by the donor himself. For those with limited information, the DSR is a place to post whatever you do know, and then to compare notes with others in the same situation. Because all postings on the DSR are via a username that you choose, your privacy is protected until you make the affirmative choice to share your personal information with someone else through a confidential message. Choose a username that is unique to your postings on the DSR, a name that can't be googled and easily traced back to you. If you're not quite ready for contact, you don't even need to add a posting in order to keep track of how many other families there are and the ages of children posted for your donor number.

HOW TO USE THE DSR

1. Log on to www.donorsiblingregistry.com.

2. Learn your way around the DSR. Browse the Web site's help page, articles, success stories, research, and information.

3. Join the Yahoo! discussion group. From the DSR home page, click on the link for the DSR's Yahoo! Group and

sign up to read and participate in the discussions with other group members.

4. Request a free consult. Wendy can provide coaching on any number of issues, or you can talk to a licensed therapist.

5. Access information. You can search by clinic or you can browse through the postings, which are messages that both visitors and members can view. If you know your facility name and donor number, check to see if you already have any matches on the site. If you have limited information, search for postings that include whatever you do know—location, dates, or donor details.

6. Register for membership and a username. You can pay for a year's membership or for a permanent membership. Those under the age of eighteen must join and post with their parents, per the User Policy. A membership allows you to add a posting and contact other members.

7. Add your posting by clicking on the "Add a New Posting" tab. The site walks you through the process. Add as much information as you like. The more information you add, the greater your likelihood of matching, especially if you don't have a donor number. Be as clear as you can about the level of contact you're seeking.

(continued)

8. Add a photo to your posting, if you are comfortable doing so. You can choose whether to have the photo viewable only by your matches or by all DSR members. If you have medical information to share, add it to the medical page that is available only to those who have posted with the same donor number.

9. Make contact! If you have matched with others who have posted for your donor number, they will be sent an automatic e-mail telling them the good news. You can also send them a message through the DSR's messaging system.

10. Use the DSR for keeping current with other families, articles, and research about donor conception.

When you enter a posting on the DSR, you will be asked to provide all the information you have about the donor. If you have a complete donor profile, then you already know the facility and donor number, and the profile may also include the height and weight, hair and eye color, skin tone, academic background, profession, and perhaps even a handwritten message from the donor. Once you've included as much or as little of this information as you would like, you can then add a personal message to your posting for other members to read. Your personal message might be short and sweet, such as "I am the mom to amazing twins. I am open to contact by half-sibling families and the donor, to whom I am most grateful!" Or your message might be more personal and revealing. Here is

Stacy's personal message, which she wrote in hopes of her donor signing on and reading it one day:

> **I MAY NEVER MEET YOU,** *but there are some things that I do know about you. I know some of these things because they are things you recorded when you donated. Then there are things that I know you passed on to me. I know that you have large green eyes that are windows into your soul, and can't keep any secrets. You have a nose that you probably weren't fond of as you grew up, but that one day miraculously seemed to fit your face just right. And you have big toes that are disproportionately large compared to your other toes, but being a guy you may not have noticed it much.*
>
> *I am thankful for all of the things I know and may know about you. And if I never meet you, they are enough. But there are some things I wish you could know about me. First, that I wouldn't change my mother's choice to have me as a single woman, nor my upbringing with her and my grandparents, nor any experience I have had thus far in my life. I know all of those things have shaped me as a person and contributed to my life, which is a blessing. But most of all, I wish you could know that I am eternally grateful for you and everything you are, and I thank you. After all, without you, there would be no me.*

Once you add your posting to the DSR, you are in the best position to be found by others. Because many people "lurk" (like Tamsin Eva, the *New York Times* essayist whom we discussed earlier)—that is, follow the site without registering or posting themselves—you might have a match even if you don't see anyone with your donor number. Some people might still be trying to get comfortable with the idea of contact, or they are simply waiting for someone else to turn up before declaring themselves. All contact is by mutual consent, so everyone who posts does desire *some* level of connection. Once they've found a potential match, some people exchange e-mail addresses and personal information immediately. On the other hand, you may feel more secure remaining anonymous until you have built up some trust with the other family through communicating via the DSR. You can get to know the other family by sharing photos, providing medical information, and even sending messages back and forth, all while retaining your privacy.

When a message is sent through the DSR system, the DSR sends the recipient an e-mail to let him know that a message awaits him on the site. Upon signing into the Web site, the recipient can access the message center and see all messages that she has both sent and received. When new matches join, or when new medical information is added for your donor number, you are immediately notified. It could happen at any time. Some people see postings from half-sibling families or even from their donors the very first time they visit the DSR—immediate success. Some will have to be more patient. The second person who posted on the DSR, right after Ryan in 2000, finally connected with her donor on the DSR late in 2012. This is a great example of why you should never give up on the possibility of connecting.

Another reason for diligently searching DSR postings is that a reported 22 to 27 percent of sperm donors say they've donated to more than one sperm bank or clinic, with some donating at more than ten or fifteen. With some sperm banks shipping vials around the world, and with different numbering systems at each bank, connecting the dots outside of the DSR would be nearly impossible. Many families have found their donors on several facility lists on the DSR by searching for characteristics listed on the donor profile. For example, searching for a six-foot, six-inch astrophysicist, rather than by donor number, allowed Louise to find her donor on three separate sperm bank lists on the DSR. If not for her diligent sleuthing, she never would have known about a dozen of her daughter's half siblings. Even though egg donors are more limited in the number of times they can donate, the DSR provides an effective forum for finding half siblings and the donor herself.

Contacting the Fertility Facility

While you are waiting to connect through the DSR, you can collect additional information to help expand your search. Offspring should check with their parents to see what help they can provide. If you are a parent who can't remember which doctor or facility you used, search the DSR's clinic listings by location to see if any seem familiar. If the doctor or clinic is still in business, check with them to see if they have any files or if it was their custom to use a particular bank. If the doctor or clinic is no longer in business, find out if the files have been transferred to another practice. Some banks and agencies are more open to providing follow-up information than others. Offspring with parents who are unable to help (or are unwilling to do so) can talk with other relatives, as they might remember the names of the doctor or clinic or, at the very least, the location.

When Ryan was seven and asking about his donor, Wendy encouraged him to write a letter to the sperm bank. Although she did not expect any additional information, and had been told that the bank would never pass the letter along, she thought that the process of writing the letter would empower Ryan by allowing him to take action and express his feelings. Here's what he wrote:

> Dear haspitl,
>
> my name is ryan. i am a doner baby. im 7 years old and my mom is wendy kramer. i have been wating to get in touch with you to find my dad. But you wont let me til im 18. i will try to keep in contackt with you to keep gettng infurmachin about my

dad like his phon number becos id like to meat him as a kid ensted of being 18. so please call or mail me with some infurmation.

ryan kramer

Wendy was right: Ryan never received a response to his letter, but some banks and clinics do respond, although they may only say that they cannot pass along messages from children to their donors. In general, if they are willing to release anything at all, then it is only to former clients, the parents, not the offspring. For offspring who need information from a clinic or sperm bank, it can be really important to share your desire to search with your parents, as they may be the ones who can actually receive the requested information from the facility. Here is a sample letter from a parent to a doctor's office that could also be adjusted for a clinic or sperm bank.

Dear Facility,

I was inseminated on [DATE] via your office and am delighted to have the chance to thank you again for your help in conceiving my precious son/daughter, who now is eighteen. When I called to let your office know that I was pregnant, I received some limited information about the donor. My child very much would like to know more. I don't want to violate the donor's privacy, but it would mean a lot to our child to know more about the donor's ancestry, looks, talents, and interests. We would like his medical history and an approximation of how many pregnancies were conceived using this donor. And we would like to meet him, if that is an option.

Any help you can give us would be tremendously appreciated. The keys to my child's genetic identity are in your hands.

Be diligent when contacting sperm banks, egg agencies, clinics, and doctors' offices. They are often hesitant to release information, even information such as the donor number that is not confidential, and often take the attitude: "Uniting donors and the families they've formed is not part of our business." They might claim that they no longer have the information you need or that all records have been destroyed. Wendy has seen the "squeaky wheels" get further with clinics and doctors' offices, so keep pressing them. Some offices have ultimately admitted that information may be available but that it is now located offsite and therefore takes more time and effort to retrieve.

Occasionally, you can get some useful information. Wendy had never seen her donor profile before contacting her clinic to learn the name of the sperm bank that it had used for her insemination. Some banks occasionally let people know whether there are any other reported births from the same donor. You might even find a sympathetic employee who is willing to provide limited help, but don't count on it. Some clinics can be convinced that releasing nonidentifying information will not violate anyone's privacy. A few sperm banks have developed their own small donor-sibling connection services or chat boards.

Unfortunately, these services are not always useful: donors aren't included, offspring themselves may not be able to register, the registries are not well publicized, and the registries are less useful if your donor provided gametes to more than one facility. As the larger sperm banks boast that they ship sperm to dozens of countries all over the world, many recipients are not even aware that their sperm originated at an American sperm bank. Frequently, people add postings for their own local clinic on the DSR, without realizing that their matches are already listed on the originating sperm bank's list. If you have used a local clinic, make sure to ask if the sperm came from a larger bank, and which one it was. You should then add postings for both your local clinic and the originating sperm bank because your matches might look for you on either list.

Attempting to get information from the doctor, clinic, agency, or sperm bank is an important step in searching, but it is often a frustrating one. Some sperm banks that offer "open" or "willing-to-be-known" donors (those who are supposedly willing to meet offspring when they turn eighteen) only send donors a generic letter in the mail, asking for "updated medical information," never mentioning that there is a donor child wishing to make contact. Most facilities will not contact donors specifically to let them know that offspring want to meet them. Many donors have tossed these letters in the trash, thinking that since they have no information to update, there is no need to contact the sperm bank. Offspring are then left to think that the donor has no desire to meet them.

This is what Leanne told Wendy:

I AM A DONOR-CONCEIVED PERSON. *I am listed on the DSR and I have found a brother, whom I've yet to meet. The reason I'm writing you is that I am also searching for my donor father. Mostly, I'm just curious about who he is, but I am also concerned about the gaping hole in my medical history. He has not updated his medical history in over twenty years.*

I wrote the sperm bank, just to see if my donor might be interested in contact. I received a reply this morning; they are refusing to even contact my donor, to at least give him the option that didn't exist twenty-six years ago.

What is infuriating is that my rights are not even considered. I have a right to know my biological father's medical history—and I believe he has the right to decide whether or not he wants contact with any offspring. But the sperm bank said it would be "too disruptive to the donor and his family" so they won't even consider contacting him.

Leanne was, understandably, quite upset and frustrated: How could this sperm bank possibly know that contact would be "disruptive" to the donor and his family? Why would they assume that all donors do not wish contact? Many donors are completely unaware that they even have a choice to connect with the children they've helped to create. Why not give the donor the choice?

Even if the bank or egg agency can't (or won't) provide any help, there are other places to look.

Swabbing Your Cheek and DNA Testing

As genetic testing becomes more sophisticated, numerous "trace-your-heritage" companies advertise their ability to help you trace your ancestry through cheek-swab cell scrapings or through spit. And they are right: they can help even if your donor and no one else from the donor's immediate family has ever swabbed their cheek.

While almost all DNA is rearranged at every generation, two pieces of DNA can help with tracing: (a) mitochondrial DNA, which is passed from a mother to her children, but which only daughters can pass on to the next generation; and (b) the Y chromosome, which is passed directly from father to son. Commercial DNA labs can use these tiny pieces of data to provide you with lists of relatives based on who else is in their database. You may learn about relatives who are closely related to you or only about more distant ones, with whom you shared a common ancestor thousands of years ago. Some labs will also tell you which diseases you may be a carrier for, and some can tell you if you have certain genes, for example, the BRCA1 and BRCA2 genes, which can indicate a higher predisposition for breast cancer. Labs can also use your DNA to give you more general information about your ancestry, such as your ancestors' countries of origin.

If you do connect fairly closely with some genetic relatives through these "family finding" DNA tests, your next step is figuring out how all these relatives fit together. When he was a teenager, Ryan found his donor through genetic testing. Looking for more information about his ancestry and countries of origin, he submitted a cheek swab and soon matched with two men at the 37-marker level, which meant that they were highly likely to be related within the previous eight generations. These men were not closely related to each other or to Ryan; however, they did share a last name, albeit with slightly different spellings. Because Ryan and these two strangers were all connected by a distant relative from the 1600s (one of the men was an active genealogist and had created a family tree stretching back hundreds of years), and because Y-DNA is inherited in the male line virtually unchanged, it was reasonable to assume that this might be Ryan's donor's surname as well. As Ryan's donor had listed English/Irish as his heritage, the last name made sense and was certainly feasible. Ryan used the birth city of the donor, his birth date, and the potential surname in an Internet search. Within days, Ryan had identified his formerly anonymous donor, despite the fact that *neither the donor nor anyone in his immediate family had ever considered DNA testing.*

Despite Ryan's success story, DNA testing is not always this likely to help you locate your donor. It may, however, turn up valuable and surprising information about your heritage. Terry, a twenty-one-year-old donor-conceived woman, found potential fifth cousins and learned that her family was from Russia before the trail went cold. Ruth, who was in her thirties and knew nothing about her sperm donor, found out that her paternal heritage was Jewish; she had always believed that her parents had asked for a donor who was, like themselves, Catholic.

When offspring match with potential donors and half siblings without the luxury of donor numbers, a DNA test is necessary. Even if you find a half sibling with a matching donor number, you may still want to confirm with a DNA test, as it has been reported publicly and privately that families sometimes receive sperm that is not from their chosen donors.

DNA testing is recommended whenever people want 100 percent assurance that they are genetically related.

Internet Searches and Social Media Web Sites

Nate was teaching himself how to use Facebook, stumbling around on his friends' pages, and not in the least looking for the egg donor who helped create his twin sons. He happened across a photo that looked familiar, and then he realized why: it matched the nameless photo attached to the anonymous donor profile. He clicked on her public Facebook page, and he found information that matched her donor profile; a few more clicks took him to her address. Obviously, this was very lucky, but others have found a match and a name simply by googling a few of the details they know, such as the donor's academic background, location, and special interests.

To come up with the potential name of your donor, make a list of all of the keywords you want to use and start searching by using different combinations. If you've kept a journal or computer file, cull this for relevant tidbits. Did the donor's profile include anything that might be unique or identifying? Did he or she win music awards, play on the hockey team, or write for the school newspaper? Is there something distinctive about the donor's parents: Was one a famous football player or writer or successful in a unique profession? Any hints as to where the donor attended college or specialty studies? How about any brothers or sisters listed? These pieces of information may lead you down the right road.

If your donor's profile provided an exact birth date and place, as did Ryan's, then you can ask an online people search company, like Omni-Trace, for a list of everyone born in that city on that particular date. Coupled with information from DNA testing, including possible last names, you might be able to locate genetic relatives that way.

Once you have a potential name, keep using search engines and social-networking sites to gather contact information. Facebook, LinkedIn, and

Classmates.com may have listings and even photos of your donor. Plug the name into Google Books to find out if your person has ever been mentioned in a book's text or acknowledgments. Ancestry.com and similar genealogy Web sites can be helpful in tracing family trees. As part of her research for this book in tracing her own family tree, Naomi searched for herself on various sites, including pipl.com and 123.com; she was amazed at the information about her life that was available, including her profession, family members' names, addresses, and phone numbers. She even found out that her mother might have had a sister whom she never knew.

Searching for Donors the Old-Fashioned Ways

Before genetic testing was possible, and before the Internet, people still had their ways of tracking down information. Even today, these methods can come in handy.

All Kathleen knew about her donor, besides the approximate date of his donation, was that he was a Baylor Medical School student and that her mother had requested someone with blond hair. In 2006, she went to Baylor's med school library and pored over yearbooks from 1979 to 1984. In the beginning, she was naive enough to think he'd jump right out. She paid close attention to eyes and smiles. She photocopied the pages and asked friends to flip through them and star the best candidates. Before she knew it, she had come up with a list of six hundred candidates, whom she alphabetized and stuck into binders. She sent letters to all six hundred of them and received responses from almost half. After sixteen DNA tests, she has not found her donor, but she has become friendly with several of the men. They call her their "collective pseudo daughter."[2] If you think that yearbooks might provide a missing clue, then you can try an online yearbook search engine.

Printed matter provides other potential search opportunities (although we've found that the Internet is far more effective). For example, donor-conceived people have advertised in newspapers. You can also plug your Internet search keywords into newspaper databases, which are especially useful for finding older information that has not yet been digitized. Public libraries usually provide access to newspaper databases, and librarians can be extremely helpful—they are information retrieval professionals, after all.

If you are bound and determined to locate your donor, and feel comfortable with finding him or her through any resource possible, you can make sure that you've left no stone unturned by hiring a private investigator. If you do, you'll want to investigate the PI's background, credentials, and testimonials. Is the PI licensed in your jurisdiction? What other kinds of investigations has the PI undertaken? What will it cost you? Talk to the PI about how she will search and what you should expect from the process. Regardless of whether the PI has access to more specialized databases, you may feel relief at turning over the search to someone who has more experience than you do in finding people. If your donor is found this way, you will need to explain honestly to him or her, at some point, about how he or she were found. If explaining that you used a PI to locate him or her wouldn't feel comfortable to you, then you should not take this step.

Finding without Searching: Random Meetings

Sometimes, there is no searching at all, just finding. When one donor-conceived teenager connected with her half brother on the DSR, they realized that she had been his summer camp counselor several years earlier. After connecting and sharing photos on the DSR, two half brothers were shocked to realize that they had been on the same Little League team when they were younger. While the genetic connection wasn't known at the time of these meetings, these offspring were, unbeknownst to them, connecting with their half siblings. Many people have told us about random meetings at parks, at school functions, at parties, and even on Disney cruises. In the course of casual conversation, donor conception comes up and connections get made. That's exactly what happened to Barbra:

> **WE WERE AT A GATHERING** *a few months ago and got to talking with a woman with a three-month-old little girl. We asked her if she went to a fertility center, she said yes and we realized it was the same one we used. We asked her what donor number she used and it was the same as ours. We couldn't believe the miracle we were experiencing. Our son had a baby sister. They sure do look alike. Although we live in separate households, we will raise them as brother and sister, considering they are both only children. We felt so incredibly blessed to have this random meeting.*

Sometimes close acquaintances turn out to be genetically related, as Maureen reported on the DSR:

> **ONLY A FEW WEEKS AFTER** *I posted that I was looking for potential siblings for my daughter (when she was about eight months old), we were contacted by the mother of a donor sibling through this site. To our big surprise, I already knew both the mother and the child. The mother and I had gotten to know each other during our pregnancies, but talking about donor conception was not something that came up during our casual conversations. Our children were born four days apart, live ten miles from each other, and have spent time together since they were born. Suddenly we understood why we were dealing with the exact same issues with the children at the time, but we would never have guessed that they had the same donor.*

Jean also reported on the DSR that she had a gut feeling that her daughter was a half sibling to a child they had recently met:

I GOT THE CONFIRMATION from the clinic today. I'm not sur-prised. The personalities are way too much alike for them not to be from the same donor. The fourteen-year-old girl lives within walking distance to my parents' home. That was scary for me. I don't mean the girl or the distance, but what would happen if a parent didn't tell their children about this and it was a boy/girl relationship. Truth is always better. I'd hate for two children to end up married only to dis-cover that they are half brothers/sisters.

Wendy knows of many situations in which families connected with their donors, only to discover that they already knew each other. In one case, the donor was a family member, related by marriage, and they all had attended family weddings together over the years, never realizing that they had this additional familial bond. A mom in another half-sibling group figured out who their donor was. When she shared this informa-tion with the group, another mother was stunned to realize that he was a college friend of hers.

When this happens, you might feel delighted and relieved, or it may make you uncomfortable as you place someone you've known in one con-text into an entirely different situation. Although donor conception is not generally something that people discuss in getting-to-know-you conversa-tions, its increasing use and visibility mean that random meetings and unexpected revelations about genetic relatives are not as unlikely as you might think. Donor-conceived teens and adults should always ask poten-tial romantic partners if they were donor-conceived. We have to face the fact that donor-conceived half siblings can, and do, meet randomly any-where and at any age.

Finding—Too Easily

Not everyone spends years searching and waiting. Some casual browsers are shocked by how quickly they come up with the identity of their "anonymous" donors, especially if they have not fully thought through the discovery's ramifications. The Internet has transformed our abilities to search and find one another, and it is challenging people's expectations of anonymity. Be careful what you wish for. While we generally think that finding members of your donor family is a positive step, not everyone is prepared. A casual search—would it be possible to find my donor?—can easily lead to more information than you might have expected. Make sure that you are emotionally ready to deal with knowing the identity of your donor and that you're prepared to deal with other issues, like whether you are ready to reach out for contact, if you will share any information you learn with other families who used the same donor, and what you will tell your children about your find.

Sondra never expected to find her donor:

MY SON AND I FOUND OUT *who our donor was by playing around on the Internet, without really thinking about what would happen if we actually did find him. By googling a few particulars in the profile provided by the sperm bank . . . there he was. It was shockingly easy, too easy really. We have no idea what we will do or if we will do anything with the information. It was, at the very least, interesting to my son to know who his bio father is and where he gets many of his skills and physical attributes. It has raised a lot of ethical issues and general confusion: Do we initiate contact? Wouldn't that be a breach of the bio father's privacy? How would we make contact? Should we let the two half sisters (recently found on DSR) know the information*

about their bio father? How do we manage the risk of making contact
and potentially having my son face the rejection? Would contact with
the bio father damage his current life situation? We are going to pon-
der for a while.

Information is powerful, and Sondra and her son can now make truly
informed decisions. They also have nothing to lose by reaching out to the
donor. (For advice on how to do this, see the next chapter.)

Donor's Rights: Is It Fair to Try to Find Them?

Peg, an architect in her late twenties, had found three of her half siblings,
and she was trying to decide whether to search for her donor. She explained:

> WHEN MY PARENTS *bought the sperm, they agreed they would*
> *never search for the donor and the sperm bank has refused to give me*
> *any further information, telling me that they protect their donors*
> *from contact. The donor has not registered on the DSR, and he does*
> *not seem to want to be identified. I still want to find out more about*
> *my missing half, but I'm not sure that it would be right for me to con-*
> *tinue searching.*

Is it appropriate for Peg to search? For many donors, the answer is yes.
They do want to be found, and they are themselves seeking out potential
offspring. There are more than two thousand egg and sperm donors who
have posted on the DSR who are now open to mutual-consent contact,
many of whom donated under the belief or promise of anonymity. They

often had no choice but to donate anonymously, or, even if they did choose anonymity, they have had a change of heart. After years of worrying that they might be legally or financially responsible for offspring that they connect with, or that these offspring will expect them to become full-time parents, many donors registered on the DSR have come to understand why offspring are so curious and what exactly it is that they are searching for. Once they feel confident that children are not looking for money, a significant time commitment, or a "dad," many come forward. They also understand that the law has protected anonymous donors and that they have no legal or financial responsibilities toward any children born through their donations.

But what about donors who have not indicated a willingness to be known, either at the time of donation or by not registering on the DSR? Some people are concerned that it is unfair to try to find these donors. They believe that most donated within a system that guaranteed them anonymity when they provided eggs or sperm. It is easy to imagine that the appearance of unknown offspring on their real or virtual doorsteps could be upsetting, or at the very least disruptive, to some of the donors and their families.

We hear you, and we agree that this issue deserves serious consideration. And here is our seriously considered response: we believe it is the right of donor-conceived people to learn as much as they can about their biological parents. Your child—or you, if you are donor-conceived—never signed any contract or made any promise not to seek out their genetic relatives (sperm banks and egg agencies only sometimes receive such promises from the parents). A donor's potential interest in anonymity should not trump the rights of a donor-conceived person to know where she came from. Many other countries have recognized the rights of donor-conceived people and do not allow donors to remain anonymous throughout a child's life, but there are no comparable laws in the United States. However, if you do find your donor, and the donor does not want any contact with you, then we also believe you need to respect the donor's wish for privacy. (We give you more advice on how to handle this situation in later chapters.)

We also believe that the benefits of searching almost always outweigh the risks. When they are found, many formerly anonymous donors do not reject contact. Often, like Rich, whom you met at the beginning of the chapter, they have wondered about offspring but are under the mistaken impression that they are forbidden to reach out in any way. Their response to being found will vary, depending on their personalities and their own emotional readiness for contact. Some, like Ryan's donor (who believed he would always be anonymous), are hesitant at first. They don't understand what kind of contact is desired or what exactly this could mean for them and their families. Ryan and his donor communicated initially through e-mail only. But then, about three months after the initial contact and feeling more comfortable, he invited Ryan to come visit him and his family. Others, like Rich, welcome contact immediately.

In fact, when offspring find anonymous donors, happy endings are common. Michelle, a waitress from Sacramento, used a donor to conceive her daughter, Cheyenne, who was born in 1998.[3] When Cheyenne turned five, Michelle joined the Donor Sibling Registry and began searching for other families who had used the same donor. She was concerned because her daughter had a sensitivity to sounds and walked on her toes, so she was interested in finding out if any half siblings were displaying similar types of behavior. Through the DSR, she was able to meet other parents and some of her daughter's half siblings. She learned that two of them had autism and that two others also displayed aspects of sensory disorder. When she called her sperm bank to find out more, the bank would not release the donor's identity. Because genetic testing is not part of the bank's protocol or required by the Food and Drug Administration, the bank could not offer any information about his genetic history, much less specifics about what might have caused these traits.

Michelle persisted. Through DNA testing, and then connecting with others on genealogy sites, she found the obituary of a former baseball manager whom she suspected might be her donor's father. This led her to the potential donor's phone number, which she called. She began to ask him questions: "Was your father in the Baseball Hall of Fame? Were you born in Illinois? Did you ever donate sperm?" When the man said yes, she asked him to confirm his birth date. He did, and she burst into tears. "You're the biological father of my daughter," she said. He was shocked but agreed to talk to Cheyenne on the phone—and eventually allowed the mother and daughter to visit him in Los Angeles. Michelle also told him about his other offspring, and the relationships among the donor, Michelle's family, and several other families continue to unfold.

We can't promise that your donor will respond like Ryan's donor, or even like Cheyenne's donor. If you find the person you believe to be the donor but he denies ever having donated, or if he acknowledges his donation but refuses to acknowledge you, then you'll need to respect that person's desires, frustrating as that may feel. If you find a donor who is not initially interested in contact, give him some time to adjust to this new reality of offspring, as he may eventually change his mind. In the meantime, you will still have learned much from the search. You may have been able to gather medical information or even connect with other members of the donor's family.

Whatever the outcome, you should not feel bad about trying to flesh out your origins. As Roger, a donor-conceived person, emphatically explains:

NO ONE EVER ASKED ME *if I wanted to be born without knowing my biological father. We know that genetic relations do not guarantee ideal parenting or family environment. But we also know that genetic connections are important anchoring points for an individual. The United Nations Convention on the Rights of the Child, sanctioned by all 190 members of the United Nations except the United States and Somalia, acknowledges, in articles 7 and 8, the right of the child to preserve his or her identity, including nationality, name, and family relations as recognized by law without unlawful interference. Even though I recognize the complications it can bring to family life when contact with a donor is made, I strongly believe it is my right to negotiate those connections.*

Time to Stop?

At some point, after you have found no one and you've tried everything from registering on the DSR to cheek swabbing, you may feel that you have no further search options. Instead of driving yourself crazy trying to come up with new strategies, it's important to recognize that eventually your search will have to come to an end—or at least a temporary stop. Naomi's husband, Tony, who was adopted, stopped actively searching for his biological father after scouring employee records for the business where his father may have worked, after hiring a private investigator, and after DNA testing, all of which yielded no further information. He feels that additional efforts would likely be futile unless he comes across new data. Although Tony wants to know more and he wonders about attributes and medical conditions he might have inherited from his biological father and passed on to his children, he recognizes that he needs to focus on other areas of his life.

While a posting on the DSR always leaves you open for potential contact, once you've stopped actively searching, you probably won't look for matches every hour or day; instead, you'll check back once a month or so. Just remember to keep your contact information up-to-date. Similarly, if you've done a DNA test, you can wait for notifications of new DNA matches or log in every few months to see if there are any new relatives who have also submitted their cheek swabs.

chapter eight

A Match! What Happens Next?

Sometimes we do a thing in order to find
out the reason for it. Sometimes
our actions are questions, not answers.

· JOHN LE CARRÉ ·

"My beautiful, loving, compassionate son has a sibling! I am still absorbing the wonder of this. When he was young he wanted a sibling very much, and I was not able to give that to him. Wow; he is not so alone anymore."

—*Martha, mother*

"Found my donor! I logged onto the DSR with really low expectations of actually finding him (or donor siblings) but I ended up finding him AND donor siblings! GOOD LUCK—:) DONT GIVE UP!"

—*Nicholas, donor-conceived person*

"At the time I was involved in the donor program, I wanted anonymity. Since then, however, I've come to believe that 'the keeping of the secret' is profoundly wrong for many different reasons, not the least of which is the perverse 'it's just bodily fluid' argument. It most assuredly is not. Consequently, though I still respect deeply the right of privacy for parents and their donor offspring, I no longer think privacy is my claim to make, and I can't wait to meet my donor daughter!"

—Jack, donor

This is what you've been waiting for: you've found your donor, or a half sibling, or offspring. You may be jumping up and down, trying through laughter and tears to read the message about the person you've found and thinking that this is the most amazing moment of your life. Or you may feel a little panicked as you realize what a profound effect this could have. What are the next steps to take?

First, try to take a deep breath. While many people do feel instantaneously joyful and ready for contact, some have more complicated reactions. This moment can bring up emotions you had not anticipated when you first started searching. You don't need to respond immediately. Social worker Liz Margolies advises DSR members not to rush into contact at this point: "It is critical to move at your own pace and to move ahead slowly."

Once you've managed to take a (tiny) step back, decide what you want to do next. Do you want to make contact now? If so, how? Would you prefer to wait? Do you want or need to discuss your course of action with your partner or other family members before doing anything further?

It is perfectly natural, even at this point, to feel ambivalent about establishing a relationship with your donor, half siblings, or offspring. Whether you are a parent, a donor, or a donor-conceived person, the strong desire to find genetic relatives can exist alongside an intense fear of the ways these new connections might disrupt your life and your family. Try not to push yourself. Remind yourself of why you started searching in the first place and what you are seeking. Our best advice is to follow the old carpenters' adage: "Measure twice, cut once." That is, think carefully before you act.

When you move forward, remember that no two connection experiences are alike—not for other families who have connected, and not for you either. Each person you meet will be coming with her own set of expectations, personality, and family dynamics. As you connect with each new match, you will ease into the process and become more comfortable with meeting new people that you'll likely know for the rest of your life. Before you send an e-mail responding to your very first match, let's explore some of the possible reactions you might be experiencing.

Feelings about Moving Forward

Here is how Betsy, the mother of a donor-conceived child, explained her feelings about her first meeting:

> **AT FIRST I WAS NERVOUS.** *Did I really want to make contact with anyone? My life with my daughter was wonderful. Why mess it up? It was a scary few days after that initial e-mail. Then I realized I wasn't messing anything up, what I was doing was giving my daughter an extended family. Our meeting this past March was like a beautiful dream. Our daughter and her East Coast half sister melded*

together like peanut butter and jelly. There was something inde-scribably wonderful about watching half sisters get to know each other in person for the first time, and really enjoying each other and their special bond. They had so much trouble saying good-bye that we extended the stay by having a sleepover that night. If it were up to the girls, they would have extended the visit even further.

The prospect of meeting people whose children share half of their DNA with yours can be very exciting, and you may be looking forward to expanding your family and community through these new virtual connections. When that first message from a match arrives, you know the search has been worthwhile, and you expect that your family's life is about to change for the better. While you have no idea about what will happen next, many people can't wait to find out and are ready to continue the connection process. If this is you, act on those feelings, send the first e-mail, and trust that your match will respond.

Some people do nothing further after discovering a match, deciding to save this information until their children are old enough to decide for themselves what to do. For example, one mother registered on the DSR to find out if her seven-year-old daughter had any half siblings. Although she found four, she didn't reach out to connect because her child had not yet asked about them. But she explained, "If she wants to find them I know how to contact them."[1] If you are considering this path—finding your child's half siblings but neither connecting them nor telling your child—try to imagine what will happen when you finally do tell. Your child is likely to wonder why you kept this information from her, denying her the opportunity to know about and to connect with these half siblings, or even her biological parent, when she was younger. She may feel betrayed, or be disappointed and angry that she missed out on growing up with these genetic relatives. Greta, now a college senior, found out when she was thirteen years old that her mother had been in touch with five half siblings—for years—before telling her. Even though her mother carefully explained that she had wanted to wait until Greta was ready for this information, Greta felt furious and betrayed by her parents for keeping this from her. She couldn't wait to meet her half siblings and to see what they all had in common. While Greta's mother has now apologized for not telling her daughter as soon as she established the connections, and Greta has forgiven her, Greta still wonders what it would have been like to grow up knowing her extended family.

You've already dealt with hesitations about searching and have decided to move forward; you're facing similar hesitations now that you've found this information, as you decide whether to reach out. To avoid regret about withholding information from your child, seriously examine your reasons for deciding not to reach out at this point. Is this about your child's choice, or is it really about your own or your partner's fear of connecting? This is a critical distinction that you need to face and work through. Remember that you may not have the opportunity to contact these people in the future. They may no longer be interested (something we've found as sibling groups get larger and the families and the donor feel overwhelmed), or you might not be able to find them again (they may have removed their posting from the DSR or let their contact information get out of date). This may be the only chance you and your child have.

Managing Other Reservations

When Sonia first saw a half-sibling family match on the DSR, she was excited, but she worried that getting to know new people might dilute or compromise the uniqueness and preciousness of her own children. She was also concerned that she might be inviting "craziness, clinginess, and homophobia into our lives." Looking back, she is delighted that the gatherings have had quite the opposite effect, explaining, "Each time I am with donor-sibling families, the uniqueness and preciousness of my own children is amplified by the number of children in the room and then some."

Many parents worry, as Sonia did, that managing a new network of relationships will complicate life unpleasantly. Other parents can't help imagining that their children will be so excited about the donor that they themselves will become second fiddles. Don't let these worries paralyze you. Yes, these new relationships will require some thought, and you may be confused as you try to define what they mean to you and your child. But remember that they need not, and probably won't, dominate your life in the long term. Instead, most people find, as Sonia has, that these new relationships weave into and enrich their lives, even if the initial maneuvering seems daunting.

In a study of almost six hundred members of the Single Mothers by Choice organization, most of the families who had made contact had exchanged e-mails or photos, and only about one-fifth had met in person or even talked by phone. (Logistics may also have played a role: matches can be anywhere in the country, and even around the world, making it hard for families to meet in person.)[2] As the researchers note, "Posting pictures or notes to a group carries relatively few risks. . . . The Internet is a buffer and a facilitator that allows for brief snippets of the other families' lives."[3] Many people decide that this is precisely what they want: knowledge about other families and the ability to stay in sporadic touch, rather than more intensive relationships.

If you can't shake the worry that your children will develop a strong connection to people with similar physical attributes and a shared heredity, remember who you are and how much your child loves you. You are the parent who rocked your infant to sleep, the one who watched him take his first steps and say his first words, the one who got him to school on that first day (and every day thereafter). No one can replace you. Your reaction to his moving forward can bring you closer or push you apart, and it is your choice on how to respond. You can support your children in developing this connection, secure in your own place in your child's world, and acknowledging that the bonds of both nature and nurture play vital roles in his life. Once the contacts actually start, as you become more accustomed to getting to know these other families, this should all become easier and feel more familiar.

Donor-Conceived People Connecting

Fifteen-year-old Zachary's first message to his newly found half brother: "My name is Zachary, and we share a donor. This feels sooooo amazing! But it is also really awkward. I'm not sure where to go from here, but I'm really thrilled to know I have a brother!"

If you are a donor-conceived person, your pure excitement about finding biological relatives probably coexists with other, more complex, emotions. Like Zachary, you may feel somewhat awkward: How many of us have experienced striking up a relationship with a complete stranger who happens to be a close relative? Understand that the "stranger" is probably having the same thoughts and feelings as you and that initial contact can be somewhat awkward for everyone involved. Concentrate on making them feel accepted and getting to know them, which will put them at ease and help you deal with your own feelings. The first exchange or meeting is usually the weirdest and sometimes even intense, but as time goes on and you get to know one another, everyone will probably be able to relax. Many people begin their relationships with euphoria and, over time, they experience different stages, evolving to a place where everyone feels comfortable. Your connections, feelings, and relationships are never static. They are fluid and will certainly change over time.

When seven-year-old Michael first met Josh, a half sibling a year younger than he was, Michael excitedly told his mother, "Josh is like the brother I always wished for." The funny thing is, at that point, she had not yet revealed to Michael that Josh was his half brother. His mom has reveled in the kinship that she feels with many of the other mothers in her large half-sibling group. In fact, as she told Wendy, all the moms had joked that because of the sheer size of their group, no matter where their kids went to college, odds are that they would be near *someone* in their half-sibling family.

Over time, you will figure out the significance of these new relationships and how to integrate them into your life. You may not know many other donor-conceived people, and you may be relieved not just to find the biological connection but also to find someone who has dealt with similar issues of identity and these types of family dynamics. Half siblings may feel like friends or cousins, and many on the DSR have explained that the relationship falls somewhere between full siblings and cousins, "like a sibling, once removed." Others feel like they are distant relatives or acquaintances. In a large study on donor offspring, half siblings most often described their relationship as feeling like "brothers and sisters." A lot can depend on how much you have in common with your newfound family. Just like siblings in traditional families, you might feel closer to those with whom you share interests and perspectives.

Contact with your donor can arouse a similar range of feelings. This is the note that Susie wrote to her donor:

DESPITE LIVING AN AMAZING *and beautiful life, there was always a bit of emptiness that no one could ever truly fill but you. I have finally found the missing piece of the puzzle. When I saw your* *posting on the DSR and realized that you were my father, I felt such euphoria that I barely even knew what to do with myself. I just wanted to scream and share the news with everyone! I'm so happy that I found you because you are my blood and a huge part of me.*

Connecting with a donor can be a lot harder than getting to know your half-sibling families; you may feel more pressure connecting with someone whom you feel is more like a parent than a peer. While many offspring say that their donor is like an "acquaintance," others think of the donor more like an uncle, and some offspring do end up calling their donors "Dad." Ryan was asked to categorize the relationship that he has with his donor: Was it like a father, an acquaintance, an uncle, a close relative, a distant relative, or a stranger? Ryan responded, "None of the above. There is no word to define the relationship. It's incomparable to any other relationship. It's unique." It's a different experience for everyone, and offspring can define these relationships in a variety of ways, using many different terms at different times in their lives.

Preparing to Reach Out

At this stage, some of your earlier fears about starting your search may resurface. Before making contact, think about all of your potential reactions and concerns, and talk to your parents, siblings, and other supportive figures. You probably won't manage to anticipate everything, but this preparation will serve you well when your hazy dreams become reality. Talking with others who have been through this experience might also help.

As you think about reaching out, you might be worried that these new family members won't like or accept you or that you won't live up to their expectations. Keep in mind that your new half siblings or your donor will not be focused on your shortcomings, however large they loom in your mind, just as you're not focused on their shortcomings. They probably share both your nervousness and your joy at connecting. They will want to learn about you, discovering both your commonalities and your differences—that's why they're reaching out or responding to your messages. We can't promise that contact always goes smoothly, but a fear of critical judgment should not prevent you from moving forward. Be confident that you'll be able to handle whatever comes next, just as you do in the rest of your life. Remember that their reactions have more to do with their own personalities and place in life than with yours.

You might fear that you have found someone who wants to be your best friend when all you want is to be Facebook friends. Or you might be worried about developing bonds too quickly and then being disappointed. Again, the other person might have those same fears. Each of you needs to communicate your expectations clearly right from the start. Taking it slowly helps too because it gives you time to adjust to this new relationship and to figure out what it really means to you. If it turns out that you do have differing expectations for what your relationship should be, then you can work out your differences as you get to know each other. Don't pretend to have feelings that you really don't, and don't force yourself to conform to what the other person wants.[4]

You might also be worried about hurting your parents if you put too much importance on these new relationships, even if your parents have been supportive of your search and are interested in meeting your new relations. Deal with this concern directly and explicitly, recognizing that you may be more concerned than your parents. Show respect for your parents; reassure them that there is nothing to worry about. Your new relationships have the potential to enhance, not diminish, the family you've grown up with.

If your parents have not been supportive of your search, remember that this is about you. You should still reassure them, but you are not responsible for their feelings. Reiterate your hope that they will come to appreciate your need to connect, and remind them that this doesn't affect your love and appreciation for them. While their fears could feel paralyzing to you, focus on what *you* are seeking. And, as we've said before, people's fears can dissolve as they become familiar with the unknown, so your parents may eventually (or even sooner) become comfortable with this new reality.

Donors Connecting

"My wife and I met my donor daughter and her mother last night (over dinner). It was one of the most memorable and surreal experiences I've ever had. We waited at the bar for them and just as I was relaxing, they appeared behind us. I wasn't sure my heart could accelerate that fast, but it did, even though I made it through, without CPR. I came home exhausted with happiness."

—Douglas

You may have posted on the DSR or registered with your sperm bank or egg clinic for mutual-consent contact when your offspring turn eighteen. Or you may be stunned by an e-mail or phone message from your donor-conceived offspring or a parent who has used your eggs or sperm, shattering your belief that you would remain anonymous forever. In either case, you'll need to think about how to respond.

Many donors are excited to realize that, even if they donated within a culture of secrecy, they now have the opportunity to search for and connect with their biological children. Many had no choice at the time but to donate anonymously. Some are prompted to post on the DSR due to changes in their own lives. Many donors on the DSR have said, "Now that I have children of my own, I have become interested in seeing how many other children I might have out there." Those who never started families can become curious when they read media accounts about donor conception. In fact, donors are often just as curious about the offspring that they helped to create as their offspring are about them. Like many others, Paul, who donated while a college student, is open to connecting but also respectful of the needs of his donor offspring and their families.

AS A DONOR, I'VE ALWAYS HOPED *to someday meet children born and introduce them to their biological siblings, nephews, nieces, and grandparents if they so desired. I'm open to sharing as little or as much, depending upon what the parents and/or children desire.*

I'm in no hurry and don't want to rush anything; they are in control of the experience. If and when they are ready I will be there for them as they wish. I don't want to complicate or interfere with their lives in any way. I only want to be involved to the extent I am needed in their lives. If I can bring to the children a sense of belonging, knowing where they came from and who they are, from the paternal side, I'm willing to do all that I can to help fill any voids and provide answers to their questions.

Paul's willingness to connect with donor offspring on their terms is shared by many other donors.

Advice for Donors

If you have been contacted out of the blue (not on the DSR), your initial reaction might be to respond immediately with an emphatic "no" or to delete the e-mail message without responding. You might wish that it had never appeared.

When you donated, the bank or agency may have promised you anonymity. You thought to yourself, "This is just like donating blood." You never anticipated that anyone would ever try to find you. And then, years later, you get the e-mail or phone call that makes you feel curious, angry, betrayed, or even fearful. One donor told Wendy, "As a donor I have essentially nothing to gain except the potential for an awful lot of emotional stress and turmoil. Far easier to just remain anonymous, as it was supposed to be." After Wendy explained why offspring desire contact, and how other donors' lives have been enriched by contact with offspring, he began to reconsider, and over the next few years he exchanged a few e-mails with his donor offspring. While emotional stress and turmoil are certainly possible, they are not typical; managing expectations and ensuring respectful conversations allow for meaningful connections.

In fact, once you begin to understand the reasons that offspring and families wish to connect with you, you are likely to feel much more relaxed about moving forward with contact. Numerous studies and thousands of stories on the DSR show that most people look for their donors out of simple curiosity. They don't want to invade or disrupt your life; they just want to know what you look like or whether there are any significant medical developments they should know about.

After an eighteen-year-old donor offspring requested contact through her sperm bank, former donor Greg asked Wendy for advice: "Is it appropriate to ask the individual to write to me, telling a little bit about herself? I don't want her to feel like she has to pass some sort of test, but this is a big step toward a potentially life-changing, unknown world." Wendy's answer was a resounding "yes." It is okay to ask others to share as much as they are comfortable with about themselves. The more information each person can offer about himself or herself, the higher the comfort level. This doesn't mean revealing deep secrets at the beginning (although that may come later); it means sharing about yourself—your interests, school studies, hobbies, musical tastes, sense of humor—and, most important, explaining your reasons for searching or making yourself available to be found, and how you'd like to lay the groundwork for a developing relationship. Removing the mystery of who they are is a great first step in exploring what type of ongoing relationship you're looking to establish. Out of respect for the family of his donor daughter, it was also important for Greg (and his wife) to know that the child's parents were on board with the contact. So, in his first e-mail, in addition to asking his donor daughter to tell him all about herself, Greg asked her to include information about whether her family was supportive in this decision to reach out to her donor.

You are probably worried about how contact will affect your current or future family, especially if you, like many other donors, have never told your family that you donated gametes. In this case, connecting with off-spring might necessitate several enormous revelations to your loved ones: "I was a donor!"; "I have children out there!"; and "I have connected with them!" Scary as this may seem, our position is still that more honesty never hurt a family. If this doesn't quite persuade you, consider how important it is for you to be the one who shares this information with your family: you don't want to leave open the possibility, however unlikely, of offspring contacting your spouse or children directly, or posting on Facebook, before you've spoken.

Donors who are not yet married or partnered need to think through how they will reveal information to those whom they are dating. Is this "first-date" information, or maybe third- or fourth-date information? How might potential partners feel about your already having children out there in the world? Some donors have held back making contact, afraid that they will be less desirable marriage partners if the truth gets out about the number of biological children they may have and are already in touch with.

When the time comes to incorporate these new connections into your current life for maximum enhancement and minimum disruption, the DSR community can help. Chatting with others or simply reading their descriptions of the solutions they've found will make the task seem less daunting. When you respond to your offspring or their families, it is important for you to be as clear as possible about what, if any, level of connection and ongoing contact you want. You have to decide what you feel comfortable with and what you can manage. You might ultimately decide to be quite cautious, answering only basic questions while remaining anonymous on the DSR. Or you might let everyone know that you are looking forward to those Disney World vacations with your current family and your donor-conceived families.

Your decisions will also affect the children you already have: your donor children are your children's half siblings. You need to consider the rights of your own children to know about, and connect with, their half siblings. Research on sperm donors[5] tells us that 70 percent of sperm donors' children would indeed be interested in meeting their half siblings, the people conceived via their dad's sperm donations.

There could, of course, be more than one family looking for you. You might have donated several times per week over a period of years to different sperm banks, and each donation could have been broken into twenty vials that found their way into numerous families. The thought of managing relationships with anywhere from a few to hundreds of children is understandably overwhelming. Donors who anticipate finding only a few offspring (many have been promised erroneously by their sperm banks that no more than ten or twenty children would be created from their donations) are much more likely to be open to contact than those who fear hundreds. If you open yourself to contact and find more offspring than you can handle, you will have to find your way forward, and the DSR can help you do so.

If, for example, you come to the DSR and find seventy offspring waiting, your posting can stipulate that you are available to answer questions by e-mail but that, for the moment at least, no other contact will be possible. The families will respect your needs. They will understand the challenges of connecting with so many families, as many of them are in the same position with their half siblings. Most will be delighted simply to know that you are now available to answer questions and to update medical information. As with all connections, we recommend that donors take it slowly, connect with the families when they are emotionally ready, respect boundaries, and be open and honest in communicating expectations.

How to Communicate with Your Donor or Half Siblings

The first rule for connecting is to be honest. The second rule is to be yourself. Beyond that, your expectations and contact strategy will depend largely on how you found the match: through the DSR or if your donor was willing to be known when you turned eighteen, or by sleuth work that has identified donors who may be surprised to be found. When you compose your first communication to a mutual-consent-contact match (such as ones you have found on the DSR), honestly express your level of interest while letting them know you'll respect their desired level of contact. If you like, you can offer some information about yourself to see what kind of response you receive. Make your note thoughtful: let them know how you feel, what you need, and why this is so important to you. If contact is made through the DSR and the other person has not posted photos on the site, you can ask if he would be willing to do that. Ask if there is any medical information that he would like to share with you. Share any medical information about yourself (adult offspring and donors) or your children (parents) that would be helpful for the other person to know about. If you are a parent or offspring contacting a donor for the first time, make very clear what you are *not* looking for: money, great demands on time, or disruption of his family.

FIRST CONTACT

- Start by offering some information about yourself, such as your age, your family makeup, interests, activities, and physical attributes.

- Be clear about your expectations, remembering that it is better to start off slowly.

- Frame questions gently, letting him know that you respect his privacy.

(continued)

> ☀ Be yourself!
>
> ☀ Read the e-mail several times before sending it, and think about how you would respond if it were sent to you.

If you ask questions, make space for the other person's ambivalence about contact and sharing personal information. You might confront that potential ambivalence directly by asking, for instance, "Do you feel comfortable sharing details about your current living situation?" Some people lay out their lives immediately, while others feel more comfortable sharing information incrementally, as they build trust.

Allow yourself time after each exchange to assess your comfort level and that of the half sibling, parent, or donor. If the other person is not in a position to react in a way that satisfies you, take comfort in the fact that you have opened up the possibility of communication, whether now or later. Forging these relationships is a *process*, and it almost always requires patience. We always recommend permitting donors to take the lead in determining the speed and depth of the communication because they may be dealing with reactions in their own families, as well as with other donor offspring—all at the same time.

Whether you've found your donor, other parents who've used the same donor, half siblings, or your offspring, you should reassure them that you're willing to move forward with the relationship at whatever rate feels most comfortable to them, that you don't expect them to turn their lives upside down, and that you simply want to ease into some communication, if they're amenable.

It's also critical that you adjust your expectations as you learn more about what the other family wants; you don't want to set yourself up for failure. You are opening a door, but that doesn't mean that your new family members will come running through it. They may not be in a position to react in a way that will satisfy you. As you now know, having examined your own feelings and situation thoroughly, there could be any number of reasons that they are not prepared to connect at the level you desire.

Here are some sample initial e-mails that clearly express the sender's personality and interest as well as respect for the other person's privacy. The level of formality is up to you.

To Half-Sibling Families

* From Parents to One Another:

Lisa: I'm so excited to find someone with a connection to my little boy! I would love any communication you're willing to do because I'm completely open about wanting him to have connections to siblings.

Dina: My daughter, Zoe, shares the same donor as your children. She was born several months ago, and she's a happy and healthy little girl. She has blue eyes and once she gets some more hair, I'll be able to tell you what color it is! I'm interested in making contact and sharing information so that knowing will have always been a part of her life experience. I know every family is going to be different in how they want to handle this unique situation that we find ourselves in and I will certainly respect those boundaries. This is all uncharted territory for me, and I'm not exactly sure what to say. If you would be interested in corresponding, I would love to hear from you.

Susie: Fairly new to this and a bit nervous. My husband and I are parents of a magical nine-year-old girl born in August of 2002. She is lively, wonderful, and very bright. My daughter has expressed an interest in getting to know some of her half siblings.

* From a Teen to Half Siblings:

I just kinda stumbled onto this site. I've never really thought about it but I could have siblings out there. I'm a seventeen-year-old boy with two lesbian parents. I live on the East Coast. I did a search and read your profile; I think we could be a match! This is a little crazy but I'm sitting here with the paperwork and sure enough . . . blood type A+, Jewish, born 1969, born in L.A., studying medicine . . . and a bunch of other stuff. E-mail me back and we can figure out if this is for real! This is so cool! I can't wait for your response!!!!

To the Donor

* From a Parent:

Hello, This is awkward for me and not really something I ever anticipated doing. However, as time passes, I become more curious about the "other half" of my boy/girl twins who are now fourteen years old. I don't know where to begin other than to ask if you would be willing to provide any current information about yourself and where your life has taken you. More important, I would like to know if you have had any medical conditions that we might need to be aware of. I can you tell you that these twins are healthy, incredibly bright, and have delightful personalities. I couldn't have asked for any better kids!

* From a Donor-Conceived Teen:

Hello! I've always wondered whether I would ever know your name or see your photo. I am so excited to see that you have joined the DSR. I would like to begin by telling you about my family and me. Then I have some questions for you that I hope you won't mind answering.

BREAKING THE ICE

In your first e-mails or phone calls, you can use this list of questions to get to know the other person. Some questions are more useful for donor-sibling families and others for the donor.

— personal facts —

Height:

Hair color:

Eye color:

Wear contacts/glasses?

Worn braces before?

Ear infections as a child?

(continued)

Distinguishing marks?

Blood type?

Allergies?

Parents' first names?

Mother's ancestors come from?

Father's ancestors come from?

Siblings' first names and ages?

— *favorites* ————————————————

Color you like to wear?

Pet?

Flower?

Fruit?

Vegetable?

Hobby that occupies your time?

Sport you like to watch?

City you would like to visit?

Meal?

Dessert?

Ice-cream flavor?

Game you like to play?

Book you would recommend?

Singer/band you listen to most?

Movie you could watch "over and over"?

TV shows you watch regularly?

interesting information

What is the story behind your name? Do you have any
    nicknames?

Do you collect anything?

What is your strangest possession?

What are your three favorite books, toys, or games?

If your house was burning down and you could rescue
    only three things, they would be:

About you, your family, and your friends:

Your three best qualities:

Special talent you have:

(continued)

Three things for which you are often complimented:

One thing you love about your parents:

A favorite memory with a grandparent:

Your parent often says:

A special family tradition:

Three traits you look for in a friend:

yes or no

Respond to the following statements with a yes or no.

You keep a diary:

You like to cook:

You like crossword puzzles:

You often have people over at your home:

You can remember jokes:

You like talking on the phone:

You are always late:

You can whistle well:

You bite your fingernails:

You generally save letters and postcards:

Your earliest memory:

Describe your first paying job:

The memory that still makes you laugh:

Your best birthday:

Your favorite school moment:

A smell that reminds you of your childhood:

How to Contact an Unsuspecting Donor

You've just found the person you think is your donor and have decided you want to make contact. There are several ways you might do so: letter, e-mail, phone call to business or home, perhaps even a private message or text through Facebook or another form of social media. The least intrusive way of contacting the donor is with e-mail or a letter because they give the donor private time to react rather than requiring an immediate response.

Compose your missive carefully. If you hope to get to know each other and to build a real relationship, be straightforward about that. At the same time, make clear that you are prepared to be sensitive to the donor's needs and boundaries. Here too (or here especially), be clear about what you are not looking for: money or drama. Make clear your respect for your donor's established life. Make sure to express your willingness to proceed slowly and within boundaries of the donor's choosing.

SAMPLE LETTER

*From a Donor-Conceived Person to a Donor, Located by Other
Means Than the DSR (Without Mutual-Consent Contact):*

Dear ____,

My name is Andy, and I am a college sophomore studying anthropology. Recently, I have been doing some research trying to complete my family tree. As you will understand in a moment, I have been missing a large chunk of my ancestry. You might want to sit down for this next part.

My parent(s) used donor conception in (year) and bought sperm from (sperm bank). They used donor number xxxx. I believe that you are that donor, which would make you my biological father.

It's very difficult to know what to say in this letter, as I certainly don't want to cause problems in your life. I can appreciate that this news may come as a great shock to you, and you may be wondering how it will all turn out. I am also aware that your family and friends may not know about me and that this may pose great difficulties for you. I'd like to reassure you that I have thought long and hard about writing this letter, and I would never disturb your privacy by turning up unannounced.

Let me tell you what I am not looking for. I am not looking for a "dad," or money for college. I am not looking to invade your life or take up your time. I don't wish to disrupt your family in any way. I just want to give you the opportunity to know who I am. Let me tell you a little bit more about myself. [Fill in a few important details about your life.]

I have many questions about my background, ancestry, and medical history. I was hoping that we could exchange letters and perhaps have a phone call or meeting in the future, but only if you are willing. I will certainly respect any decision you make about this, and understand that you may need some time to think it over.

Please write whenever you feel ready to do this. Even if you do not wish to have contact, it would be helpful for me to hear that. I am content to wait but really need to know your wishes. I will respect whatever level of privacy that you desire. The ball is in your court.

Sincerely,

Waiting for a response to your letter can be an anxious time. A lack of response doesn't mean a lack of interest. Your donor might just need some time to figure out how to handle this new and unexpected situation. He or she may need to talk to his or her family or feel it necessary to confirm the kinship with the sperm bank or egg clinic that he or she donated to. If, after several weeks, you have heard nothing, send a follow-up to confirm that the original message was received. In your follow-up, you can mention that you understand that your donor might need more time, and reiterate that you're open for contact whenever your donor is ready. Make sure he or she knows that it is up to him or her to take the next step.

How to Set Up Initial Meetings

After a series of e-mails and Skype or phone calls, you and your new kin may decide to meet in person. Plan the meeting carefully in order to make it a positive experience for everyone. If young children are involved, the adults may decide to meet first on their own. When children come along, there should be some activity to focus the group, whether you meet in a private home or at a park or other public spot. For example, you could plan a potluck and, depending on the ages of the children who are involved, craft activities or board games. When Ryan met his first half sibling, they went to a park and then to lunch at a restaurant. His first meeting with another half-sibling family was a barbecue at someone's home; they played games to get to know one another better.

Planned activities take away the awkwardness of everyone just sitting around staring at each other. One teen said that the first meeting was uncomfortable: "We all sat there, and our parents just stared at us. All they want to do is gawk at the eyes, the shape of the face, the teeth, the smile, because they're amazed to meet strangers who share these features with their child. But we'd rather be doing something that lets us get to know each other." At an amusement park, children can go on the rides or play miniature golf while the parents chat. Even when families live on opposite sides of the country, they can meet at each other's homes or at some middle point. If you've already had lots of phone or Internet conversations, you might even plan a beach or theme park vacation together. While this may feel like too much too soon for some people, others are excited about spending this much time together.

These first meetings can be quite emotional. Prepare for laughter, tears, and hugs. Don't forget your tissues or your camera!

"I just found out about a month ago that my dad wasn't my biological dad. I've already found three half siblings. I spent the day with two of my siblings last week. It was really fun and cool to know that I have siblings out there that look like me. It was a blast and we all had a great time.

"My family and I set up a date next week to meet my biological dad or, as you may call him, the donor. I am really excited and can't wait to meet him. My real dad and my mom are coming along too, as well as my twin sister and one of my half siblings that I already met.

"This whole experience was great and added a whole new adventure to my life."

—*Megan, thirteen-year-old donor-conceived child*

You may be delighted to discover what you have in common with the other families. In fact, sociologist Rosanna Hertz found that families bond around their "shared values" and other similarities.[6] Meetings work out most happily when we come with open hearts and few expectations.

"I made contact with three other moms. Oh, it's a brave new world! Three of us are single mothers by choice, and the fourth has a husband who is infertile. Two of the moms sent photos, and one of the mothers, Claire, was interested in further contact. She has a little boy named Luke, who is four months younger than Olivia. We corresponded for some time and had a very interesting exchange of photos and observations about our children. Finally, we decided to meet Claire and her son, Luke.

"As we parked in front of their house, my heart was in my mouth. I knew what a big milestone this was in my daughter's life, even if she didn't yet. We all had tears in our eyes as we introduced ourselves. There was such a feeling of love present for our children, these beautiful children who dashed right off to play with toys, leaving the adults to feel their way carefully along in conversation together.

"It was a wonderful visit. I had tears in my eyes again as I watched my daughter with her brother for the first time. My daughter has straight blond hair, Luke has brown curly hair, and both are darling sweet-faced children. Seeing them together, it was easy to see they could be brother and sister, but the resemblance wasn't so strong that I would pick them out of a preschool class as siblings. Their similarity is more in their easygoing and affectionate manner.

"Claire had kindly laid out an array of food and hot drinks. As we were in the kitchen together, she said, 'This must be the first time in history that two women who have a child by the same man are glad to meet.' We had a good laugh about the strangeness of it all. We visited and ate and relaxed, watching the two siblings play."

—*Debbie, mother of a donor-conceived daughter*

Meeting a donor or a half sibling is a major event, but it is not a one-shot deal. These are people whom you will probably know for the rest of your life, regardless of what happens during this first get-together. Many will share in graduations, weddings, and other life events. Relationships unfold over time, and patience is often rewarded. It's good to start out at a place where everyone is comfortable and then build from there. Take it slow. Expect bumps in the road. It's a marathon, not a sprint.

chapter nine

Beyond First Contact: Bumps in the Road

Challenges are what make life interesting;
overcoming them is what makes life meaningful.

· JOSHUA J. MARINE ·

Firstcontacts are not just about how you reach out to your donor and half siblings. They are also about starting to figure out how you will handle your new relationships. You'll be making sure that your own family feels comfortable, deciding how you will tell others, learning how to deal with the differences among families, and, perhaps, handling rejection. You can expect to face some challenges. While the bumps in the road we explore in this chapter may slow you down or create temporary diversions, you should trust yourself to be able to successfully move beyond them toward the relationships that you have hoped for. This is an important and sensitive time for all involved, so you need great care, patience, and receptivity when responding, no matter how excited you are.

Dealing with Your Family's Reactions

Making that first contact affects you as well as those around you. You'll need to deal with the reactions of different family members to your initial contact. They may be as thrilled as you are, so you may simply be deciding how to coordinate meetings at convenient times and to include everyone who is interested. But this could involve facing the potentially conflicted feelings of a nonbiologically related parent or of siblings in your own family who have different donors or are not donor-conceived.

For some families, making contact with a donor or half sibling might mean that you will now have to explain donor conception to family members, such as aunts, uncles, and grandparents, who had not known previously. We strongly urge you to consider disclosing the truth to them before you start your search, so that if and when you find genetic relatives, you'll be in a better position to unfold that piece of news without having a potentially shocking backstory to go with it.

When a Nonbio Parent Meets His Child's Half Siblings or Donor

Your child is now connecting to others with whom she shares something she doesn't share with you: genes. Stay self-confident in your own worth as a parent; your child will look to you for love and support. Focus on her and revel in the fact that she has the opportunity to learn so much about herself. The more you can embrace the other family (or families), the more enriching the experience will be for everyone involved.

"The better the relationship between the nonbiological parent and the child, the better it should withstand this test, as it were," explains Dr. Ruth Shidlo, a clinical psychologist in Tel Aviv. "Some families have found that meeting the donor relations (e.g., donor) may actually have a positive effect on the relationship between the child/adolescent and the nonbiological parent. The unknown tends to loom large on the horizon, and provides fertile ground for one's imagination. Actual contact with a real person has the power of demystifying this process." In other words, don't let your fears of the unknown stop you. The reality is likely to be quite different and constructive.

The father of one of Ryan's half sisters said that he had initially been hesitant to meet Ryan. Five minutes into their very first meeting, though, he said that he felt a great sense of relief, realizing that this was a positive experience for his daughter, his wife, and himself. Once he understood that Ryan was not in any way a threat to his own familial relationships, he became open to meeting more of his daughter's ever-expanding biological family.

Maggie, who used donor sperm, reported that her husband had consistently resisted telling their children anything about donor conception. He was opposed to disclosure and then, once the children knew, he was hesitant and fearful of contact.

MY HUSBAND DIDN'T WANT *to tell the kids. Basically, I researched positives and negatives (via the DSR), discussed them with him, and then brought it up again several months later. Eventually, he agreed. He was more adamant about not telling them about half siblings, but when I got a grudging "do whatever you want" from him, I ran with it. We have made contact and, in most cases, formed good friendships with quite a few half-sib families. At first, my husband went along to guard the kids like a pit bull, but soon he realized that the whole experience was good for our children, and he relaxed. While he is still a little worried about his relationship with our children, he is now able to focus on how important this is for them.*

Many nonbiological parents have reported similar worries about meeting their children's half siblings or donors. This is entirely normal. What's most important is to move beyond this uncertainty, recognizing it without letting it stop you, in order to allow your children the connections that are rightfully theirs. You might be surprised to find how enriching this experience can be for you. Meeting other parents who are raising children biologically related to yours can be quite rewarding and even supportive of your own parenting as you learn more about your child. Sharing experiences and finding common quirks or personality traits can be fun. Meeting the donor can allow you the opportunity to ask any questions you've had about ancestry or about medical issues. Fundamentally, these connections allow you to better understand your child.

Dealing with Difference

Families meeting for the first time may discover that their shared DNA does not always smooth over their socioeconomic, political, and religious differences. Nor does a genetic connection mean that everyone wants the same thing from contact. Negative meeting stories, which are rare, almost always arise from unrealistic expectations of compatibility and a failure to anticipate and negotiate differences. One teenage girl posted on the DSR with her mother and immediately found a half sister exactly her age. They were thrilled to have found each other, but when the first mother discovered that the other mother was a lesbian, she forbade her daughter any further communication with her new half sister. This was a heartbreaking situation for all involved. You need to be prepared to connect with people that you might not otherwise invite into your life, or else resign yourself to breaking a few hearts—perhaps including your own child's.

Families headed by two heterosexual parents are likely to connect with families headed by same-sex couples or single parents. It is okay to be unsure about the new language and relationship models they present, but you need to be ready to acknowledge them as loving family units, just like yours. Heterosexual families whose values (religious or otherwise) lead them to reject the prospect of contact with lesbian, gay, or single-parent families should probably think twice before searching for a match. As at all stages of this process, you must know yourself: if you suspect that you are not ready to be open to a family with its new-to-you demands and surprising differences, then you may not be ready to make contact quite yet. You might be connecting with people whom you normally would never have considered including in your circle of friends. Incorporating them in your family circle could be challenging. But in many ways, this is no different than a more "traditional" family—rarely do all people in *any* extended family see eye to eye on all issues.

Family structures are diverse in the donor community, and those structures may have an impact on who makes contact. Single-parent families, both LGBTQ and straight, are more likely to wish to create larger communities for their children, whereas couples, both LGBTQ and straight, seem to be more cautious about reaching out. The hesitance oftentimes comes from the nonbiological parent, be it the nonbio mom or the nonbio dad.

Regardless of family type, some parents feel a need to move forward more slowly, until they can make sense of, and better define, the best way for their family to share and integrate this information about their new connections. Remember that initial tentativeness from them doesn't mean they won't want future contact when they're feeling better prepared and after they've adjusted to the idea of including you in their lives. They, like you, are trying to make the best decisions for their children and want to make sure they are moving forward into safe territory.

Dealing with Rejection

"The donor never wrote back. It is three weeks now. I wondered for a while if the e-mail might have gone directly into trash, particularly because I used the word 'sperm.' Or perhaps, as seems more likely, the man thought, 'I didn't sign up for this' and decided to ignore the e-mail. Oh, well. I guess there's no hurry. My children are young, so he has years to change his mind . . . I hope. And at some level, just seeing his picture is enough for now. I know that he is healthy, fit, intelligent, and good-looking and that, on the surface at least, my children do not need to fear any terrible surprises as they grow older. My worry is what do I tell them in the future? When I let them know that he did not write back, that could feel like rejection, which is another difficulty for them to bear. Meanwhile, my twins continue to delight—smiling, finding their toes, realizing what their fingers are for, crawling around and rolling into each other, squealing with joy. I adore them. But his silence is painful."

—*Amy*

Sometimes, after a promising initial contact, the lines of communication go cold. A family hopes for a reply that never comes; offspring wait for responses that never arrive. You may feel rejected and wonder what you did wrong. The answer is: probably nothing. The other person's response can tell you more about them than about you. Sometimes people pull back to negotiate a plan of action with other family members. Sometimes their procrastination reflects their need to regroup and deal with their own emotions. Connecting might have brought numerous other issues to the surface, so they need time to take whatever control they can over this situation. In some cases, of course, they are feeling so overwhelmed that they may end contact altogether. Again, you need patience. Give your matched family or donor some time and space, and eventually they may be back in touch. If, after a gentle reminder, you still don't have an explanation for their silence, then you need to move on (at least temporarily) without them.

When negative experiences do happen, you can manage your response. As best-selling adoption author Sherrie Eldridge notes, the natural reaction to rejection, particularly by a birth relative, is to cease further searching and to shun support systems.[1] Instead of shutting down, continue your search and reach out to new relatives. It might be hard to do at first, but try to focus on the fact that you succeeded in finding a match. If you persevere, you will probably meet others who are willing to remain in contact.

It may be even harder for you if it is the donor who has not responded to your letter or e-mail. Try to empathize with the donor, to imagine how he or she feels. The donor could pull back, or not engage at all, for many reasons. Donors can fear the demands of unknown offspring, often because they have never received any counseling or information about these issues. They may even turn away because they feel inadequate and think they won't be good enough for the kids. They may feel ashamed that they ever donated. Or perhaps they have not told their families that they donated. In fact, while some donors feel an ethical or moral obligation to reach out to the children, they may encounter resistance from their current families. Spouses complain, "You don't have enough time for *our* family. How are you going to incorporate *these* people into your life?" In the 2011 Style network documentary *Sperm Donor*, we watched Ben and his (now) wife Lauren struggle with these issues. Lauren tried to understand Ben's interest in connecting, but found it difficult, particularly because Ben had connected with more than seventy-five donor children on the DSR. Despite Lauren's hesitations, Ben decided to continue contact, but not all donors would do so.

Prior to contact, your donor's idea of your existence was vague or non-existent, and most donors never expected any contact. Now he must adjust mentally and emotionally to a new reality—you. The donor might just need time to accept the possibility of connecting, so don't give up. On the other hand, you do need to be prepared for a donor who never responds and that is something you'll need to accept as graciously as possible. As Dr. Shidlo counsels, "Knowing that one has tried and done one's utmost, even when one has 'failed,' may bring with it a sense of closure, and circumvent the question, 'What if?'"

The Good News

If connecting with your donor or half sibling isn't the magical experience that you'd always hoped for, focus on the questions that you did have answered and the new information that you have acquired. In any family, we don't always like everything about our relatives, and we can be diabolically different from them. If you were hoping to find someone just like yourself, but found someone with completely different interests and characteristics, revel in the differences. Find peace in knowing that no matter how different they may be, they are still your biological relatives. You have still forged a connection to your genetic history that you might not otherwise ever have experienced. As time moves forward, you may come to realize that you have more in common with them than you originally thought. The more shared experiences you have with your new family, the closer you may grow to feel toward each other.

For example, teenagers who might not have that much in common with half siblings might bond later in life when they each become parents for the first time. For people who might be struggling more intensely and having a harder time reconciling the person they envisioned with reality, a few therapy sessions along the way may be helpful.

Never forget that you are not alone. Thousands of others have handled this process and successfully dealt with these dilemmas. Reach out to your support system—family and friends, your new match families, a single mothers' support group, your LGBTQ community center, or a family counselor. Even though they may not have faced exactly what you are going through, just having someone who can listen will help you to decide the best way to move forward for yourself and your family. Beyond your immediate community, you can reach out online. Families on the DSR's Yahoo! discussion group are always willing to share experiences, troubleshoot, and empathize with other families. Wendy and her licensed counselors are always available for phone consults and counseling sessions. They have lived through and have talked thousands of others through many of these sticky situations themselves.

Most initial contacts are positive, and you'll discover that people are looking forward to nurturing their new connections. Making it through some of the stresses and challenging situations that come along with this adventure—an adventure that most people outside the community of donor conception can never even begin to imagine—can enhance your life and your relationships within your family, and give you a deeper understanding of yourself and what *family* can mean.

chapter ten

Truth Is Relatives

Family faces are magic mirrors. Looking at
people who belong to us, we see the past, present
and future. We make discoveries about ourselves.

· GAIL LUMET BUCKLEY ·

Now that you've made connections, how do you move forward? The prospect of incorporating these new relationships, whether it is with one new family or a sibling group of twenty, into your current life can make you feel enormous excitement. You may also be wondering how you can possibly maintain and nurture these new relationships in your already very full life. Will you stay in touch? Do you plan yearly get-togethers? Is it holiday cards, or holiday vacations together? How can you possibly get to know twenty-five half siblings? Donors may fret about making time for new children when they already have to move mountains to focus on their children at home. They must also consider ways of describing their new "donor families" to their households, families, and friends.

While noticing your similarities and differences during a first meeting may be exciting and interesting, that's not enough to sustain a longer-term connection. Donor-family relationships, like all other relationships, take some nurturing and time, even if you just want to develop a casual friendship. Forming these relationships comes easily to some people, but others must work hard to open up, connect, and develop longer-term bonds.

"When I met my biological father, our physical similarities were probably the thing that moved me least. I discovered connections that I had never even thought about but so validated who and how I am. We attended the same type of college, have the same graduate degree, have the same kind of car, and the same habit of staying up too late at night. There are ways that he just gets me that nobody else in my life does or can. That doesn't mean he fills anybody else's role, because I have space for him in my life too. My family has really been wonderful, my mom especially. She was the one who first encouraged me to search. My dad was slower to accept the series of events, but has also met my biological father several times, and has thanked him for giving him the opportunity to be a dad. We are an evolving family."

—*Aiden*

To create longer-term relationships, you need the same openness, patience, and sensitivity that you've called on to get you to this point: you must be ready to share your thoughts and feelings openly. If the response to your initial get-togethers is an enthusiastic "How soon can we meet again!?" from all of you, then the pace will be quite different than if your response (or theirs) is a more distant "Let's talk again next year." If you have not connected through a mutual search—if, for example, you have found your donor through Internet searching or through DNA testing—then your new contacts may be skeptical about you and about further contact. Meeting their skepticism with your most authentic, open, and understanding self will help things move forward in a positive way.

As you develop these new relationships, listen as carefully as possible to the other people's needs and expectations rather than focusing solely on your own. While it might take some time to learn how to balance your own needs with those of others, it will be hard to go wrong if you truly hear your new kin. Many of you will find great joy and fulfillment as you get to know, and come to embrace, your new extended family. Of course, some of you may be disappointed that your donor is not as thrilled about contact as you are, or that your half siblings don't want to join you at the beach every summer. Nevertheless, with awareness, flexibility, and practice, you can become comfortable managing decisions that would make Emily Post's head spin.

These relationships will develop their own significance and meaning for you over time. After she met her fourth donor-sibling family, Carol explained how she felt about her connections: "Our definition of family has most definitely expanded. Since we are treading on new territory, it's still hard to know what to call these new relationships, but we know that it goes beyond friendship and leans more in the direction of family." Like Carol, you too will find your own path.

This chapter serves as a guide to establishing and maintaining relationships with multiple family members in a style and at a speed that is comfortable for you. Whether you are a parent, a donor-conceived person, or a donor, it's all about redefining family on an ongoing basis. Many people describe their donor-family relationships as lying somewhere between immediate and extended family on the kinship spectrum. Let's explore what might happen after those first few tentative contacts as people begin to discover what these connections mean to them and to their families.

Handling Logistics

There are many ways to stay in touch after a first meeting, if you decide to do so. For those of you trying to remain in contact with one other family, it will be straightforward to work out ways and frequency of communicating as your relationship develops. If you have connected with multiple others, then staying in touch can be more complicated as you navigate through numerous individuals' different preferences for how to stay connected, how frequently to communicate, and how much personal information to share. You might choose to create a group on a social media or other Web site. If your group is smaller, you'll be able to stay in touch via the DSR, private e-mails, phone, or Skype, and further get-togethers might be easier to arrange.

Larger groups may have reunions, although everyone in the group may not be able to attend. Some people have monthly dinners with other families, some go on vacations together, and others exchange occasional e-mails to give updates on important events, like graduations, or to provide new medical information or photos.

HOW CAN YOU STAY IN TOUCH?: A CHECKLIST

1. Using the DSR e-mail system or private e-mails

2. Forming a Facebook page or Yahoo! or Gmail chat group

3. Arranging phone or Skype calls

> 4. Planning yearly get-togethers on certain holidays or during summer break
>
> 5. Coordinating dinners, play dates, and other get-togethers as frequently as feels comfortable and feasible
>
> 6. Inviting one another to family events, holidays, or school events

The frequency of contact will vary, so there is no one "right" way to stay in touch. One study reported that approximately half of surveyed offspring who had found their donors or half siblings were in touch at least once a month; the other half were in contact less often.[1] As you get to know one another, you will adopt patterns that take everyone's comfort into account.

Here's how Alice, a mother who is part of a donor group with numerous members, describes their most recent reunion and the other ways they stay in touch:

WE JUST RETURNED FROM *a weekend gathering of donor siblings where nine of the twenty-three kids we now know about attended along with two single mothers, five lesbian couples, four grandmothers, and a granddad. The kids range in ages from eight months to four years. Like others, we formed a private site to share photos, etc., and have been communicating for about two years. Over the course of the past year or so, several small groups of us have met, but I must say that having such a large group was overwhelming in the best way possible. I never could have imagined how amazing this would be. Meeting the others was not only comfortable but also in-credibly natural, like we had known each other for years. The kids warmed up to one another and to the other adults immediately and the other parents seemed like old friends. Not to read too much into the genetics of it, but there was something truly special about the way everyone interacted. I can't imagine what the future might hold but I am confident that meeting the other donor siblings and their families was the best thing we could have done for our kids.*

With an Internet site, small gatherings, and an extended family week-end, Alice has found several different ways to establish and maintain strong connections with her child's donor siblings and their families. Because people may feel comfortable with different ways of communicat-ing, it's smart to allow various options within the same group. Make sure that everyone has access to the same options, and don't set up too many; you probably don't have time to respond to group e-mails along with daily checks of a DSR group and a Facebook site for new messages.

How to Manage Ongoing Connections

HOW LEVELS OF CONNECTION CAN DIFFER FOR GROUP MEMBERS

Here's one person's description of the diverse members of her half-sibling group:

Family A: very progressive; calls the half siblings "sis-ter," "brother," "half sister," etc. Has only child who is old enough to be fully aware of the group.

Family B: also very progressive and involved in keeping the group together; calls the half siblings "donor sister," "donor brother," etc. They call the donor "Donor Daddy."

Family C: very conservative, almost no interest in being a part of the group. Divorced with differing opinions on involvement with half siblings. Generally not involved with the group.

Family D: also very conservative, happy to keep up with the group, has met Family A and Family B several times. Does not use the term "half siblings" at all, instead calling them "friends."

Family E: wants to be in touch, but holds the others at arm's length. Interaction with the group is conducted on behalf of the children, to give them access and information when and if they want it. Beyond seeing their Christmas cards each year, the children know nothing about their half siblings.

When both parents and children find friendship, then connections can develop more quickly, although personalities, time constraints, travel expenses and logistics, and expectations will affect the frequency and intimacy of ongoing contact from family to family and from year to year. Tina lives on one coast and her daughter's half sibling lives in the Midwest. Distance has not, however, affected their relationship.

IN THE FEW MONTHS SINCE *meeting, our daughters, who are only a few years apart, have been sharing confidences and stories on Facebook while we mothers have been using "old-fashioned" e-mail to learn more about one another. We e-mail each other several times a week, and we've already discovered that our stories are similar, as are our daughters'. Although the entire experience is still a new one, I think both of us moms, as well as both of our daughters, are excited and overjoyed to have found one another.*

Sustaining your new relationships should be exciting, even as they become a routine part of your life. While the issues are similar for each type of connection within donor families, we explore a few wrinkles that are special to each type of relationship.

Keeping Connected: Parents with Parents

Parents who connect with one another during the donor-selection process sometimes maintain these relationships during and after pregnancy. Other parents who share donors find each other later in their children's lives. For parents, staying in touch generally supports their own interests as well as those of their children. You will develop your own ways of maintaining connections and your own vocabulary to describe your relationship with your child's donor-sibling families. One woman explained, "We are close friends who care about one another's children." Another woman called the other mothers "part of my extended family, along with their children." The terms you use can change as the connections themselves change. Another mom, Alyssa, explains:

IN OUR EXTENDED FAMILY *of donor-related sibs and parents, we moms (we all happen to be either lesbian couples or single moms) have had the deep pleasure of watching our kids forge very meaningful, fun, close relationships with one another. Their similarities and their amazing (and instant) connection and ease with one another are undeniable. These are lifelong relationships they've formed. Our relationships with our "sister moms" (for want of a better phrase . . . now there's a relationship that needs a good new label!) is enriching to us as well. Who better to understand our kids' individual and collective quirks than each other?!*

Of course, your relationships may not remind you of those with other relatives, and a monthly group e-mail may satisfy your need to stay connected. Don't feel pressure to become closer than you actually prefer. You can maintain connections without weekly phone calls and extended family vacations.

As they connect with one another, parents also focus on the importance of building half-sibling families for their children. While you may not have found any new best friends, your child may be thriving in his connections with his donor family. Gwenyth, according to a story in *O Magazine*, had searched the DSR for genetic relatives for her son, Dylan, because she wanted him to be "part of a larger community." She was successful, and now refers to the other children she found as "Dylan's siblings."[2] One mother explained the attachment that her daughter feels to her donor siblings: "There are special bonds that she is forming with them that look like nothing else I've seen with friends of hers. . . . I think she feels very full and good about herself as her experience of 'family' grows and deepens."

In the survey of almost six hundred women recruited through the organization Single Mothers by Choice, almost two-thirds wanted their "child to have the possibility of a larger extended family," and half were interested in developing a relationship with other children who shared the donor's genes.[3]

By finding genetically related siblings, parents feel that they are completing their children's communities and families. Many parents are acutely aware of the fact that they are redefining the meaning of family for themselves and for their children and expanding the reach of their kinship networks. Often parents feel a certain kinship with the donor-conceived children in other families. Although Wendy is not technically related to Ryan's half siblings, she thinks of them as family. When she looks at them, she can see parts of her son reflected in their faces, the way they walk, and their personalities.

In fact, at least one mother, Jessica, formalized her strong bond with her donor family in a legal document. "I am naming two moms (one is the alternate) whom I met on DSR as the people who will raise my son in the event of my passing. They are the mothers of two of my son's half sisters. We have spent time together, they are awesome, and I am so glad my son would be raised with a sibling (someone outside of my own nutty family, lol)." You too may want to recognize your connection legally, whether by naming someone from your donor family to serve as your proxy for health care or financial decisions or by designating that person as your desired guardian for your children in the event of your death so that your child grows up with half siblings. Of course, without taking affirmative steps to draft special documents, half-sibling families have no formal legal relationship to one another.

Keeping Connected:
How Half Siblings Stay in Touch

McKenzie tells us:

> **UPON FIRST MEETING** *my two half sisters, I had no idea what to expect. I was only eleven and had never even considered the fact that there could be half siblings out there. However, after getting to know them and growing up with them, both my brother and I have developed a relationship with all four of our half siblings. This relationship and connection with them has allowed me to understand myself better. It has opened my eyes to the fact that there is another half of my genetic identity that I'm not sure of. But instead of being dismayed by this fact, it has allowed me to appreciate the bond I share with my half siblings. Connecting with them has shown me the other half of my genetics and has caused me to truly love the fact that I was donor-conceived.*

McKenzie's half sister, Bree, describes herself as "an only child with five siblings." She adds:

> **I HAVE GAINED** *an extended family. A void I didn't know was there has been filled. My siblings have added love, caring, and support to my life, all that "sibling stuff" people normally take for granted. They are spectacular friends and people I look up to. They have defined many major events in my life; for instance, Tyler and Becca taught me how to snowboard, a sport I fell in love with and still enjoy to this day.*

For very young offspring who grow up knowing their half siblings, relationships are easy and familiar because they don't remember not knowing each other. Even older donor offspring usually have little trouble exploring and defining their new relationships. Studies find that almost all offspring who had made contact with siblings rated the experience positively. Although some simply use the DSR to share photos, send an occasional e-mail, or keep track of medical issues, many half siblings follow one another's lives, often using social media sites to stay connected. In the Emmy Award–nominated TV special *Sperm Donor*, half siblings Adrienne and Karis connected on the DSR, kept in e-mail and phone contact, and then finally met in person. They got pedicures together before Karis's senior prom and then Skyped with a half brother whom they had not yet met in person. Adrienne and Karis continue to deepen their sisterly relationship and to reach out to their half siblings.

Stacy felt an immediate bond with her half brother, Chris:

> **AT TWENTY-SEVEN YEARS OLD,** *finding a brother has been both exciting and a little scary at first. . . . After four months of talking and e-mailing from Seattle to Togo, West Africa, where he is a Peace Corps volunteer, we finally met in person a week ago. It was amazing. Like looking in a mirror but better. . . . More than one stranger has asked if we are twins! We've spent a week together now, meeting each other's friends and family, and have to remind ourselves every once in a while that we're not just good friends, but siblings. . . . It's quite the roller coaster of emotions, sudden tweaks of realization that this person is my sibling (always has been and always will be), and a sudden feeling of comfort having him there.*

Chris echoes Stacy's sentiments:

> **NEVER HAVING SEEN, LISTENED TO,** *or touched someone with whom I share a parent, I am experiencing a new strain of gene love*

for the first time. I believe I have just met my best friend as well. For me it has been healthy, enriching, comforting, and stabilizing among many other things.

This incredibly heartfelt connection shows what's possible between half siblings.

Of course, as is the case of full siblings who grow up together, inevitably not all half-sibling relationships are this harmonious. And while the bonds between half siblings take many forms, sometimes those bonds don't form at all. Half brothers Sean and Lucas connected when they were each fourteen, and they've been building a fraternal relationship ever since, even providing moral support to each other as they scheduled their driver's license tests. They have always been excited about the possibility of getting to know other half siblings. When they saw a DSR posting by the mother of a new half brother, Collin, looking for medical information about the donor, they immediately reached out, asking the mother to give Collin their e-mail addresses. Collin never responded, however, and his mother eventually wrote to let them know why: "Collin's really not terribly interested in going further in terms of meeting the other half sibs. He's more open than he has been but just isn't ready to take it any further." While Sean and Lucas initially felt rejected, they have subsequently connected with other half siblings. They now have a Facebook group with five members, and although Sean and Lucas are the most frequent posters, everyone else provides updates. After some time, Sean and Lucas have come to a better understanding of Collin's position, and they have even told Collin's mother that he is welcome to join the group whenever he is ready. As Sean and Lucas now appreciate, the desire to explore half-sibling relationships is different for each person, as is the level of ongoing connection. Make sure that you remain open to each new person and that you make space for them.

Keeping Connected: Donors and Families

Debbie, who is now in touch with her formerly anonymous donor, often invites him and his family to important family events and school functions: "Our donor and his family will be there tonight to watch my daughter's eighth-grade promotion/graduation ceremony. We are stretching the boundaries of what it means to be 'family' by allowing my donor the option of shedding his anonymity and participating in the life of a child he helped me create." Although some donors' willingness to connect goes no further than health-related questions, others want to mentor their offspring. Donor Mike, who is single, has been to one donor son's bar mitzvah, picks up another from school every day, and spends summer holidays with two of his other donor children. Donors given the opportunity to join in their offspring's lives can find the level of connection that makes everyone feel comfortable. This ongoing process requires sensitivity, careful listening, honest sharing, and, perhaps, a certain amount of negotiation with others and within oneself.

Offspring may want to establish their own separate bond with the donor rather than relying on the relationship between their parents and the donor. Although their parents chose their particular donor, offspring often view the donor as part of their own composite community and as their biological parent, not as their parents' gamete donor. They might want to communicate without parental involvement. Parents must accept their children's needs for a distinct connection, and can arrange for get-togethers that allow everyone to get to know one another better by ensuring that there is space and opportunity for one-on-one time.

Relationships with the Donor's Family

Offspring can also establish meaningful relationships with their donors' families. Many donors reach out with the support and encouragement of their partners, parents, and children. In fact, these other family members are sometimes more curious about offspring than the donor is. Sperm donor research reveals that 85 percent of their wives are open to communicating with offspring. The donor's children might also be thrilled to get to know their half siblings, eager to explore their undeniably strong genetic tie. The same research shows that 70 percent of donors' children who knew about their dad's sperm donation were interested in meeting their half siblings.[4] The DSR has postings from donors' wives, sisters, children, and parents. Some are posting with the donor sitting beside them, and others are seeking connections on their own because of their own personal curiosities or because they feel a need to share important medical information. Some post because the donor is deceased, and the families yearn to know if he left any biological children behind.

While the grandparents (donor's parents) are increasingly likely to connect while the children are young, many of their "new" grandchildren spring into their lives as older children or even near adults. Some donor grandparents are initially hesitant because of the sheer number of potential grandchildren. Others are over-the-moon happy when they hear about the existence of grandchildren. Grandparents have reported grieving for all the birthday parties, graduation celebrations, and years of casual visits that they have already missed. The biological connection may be taken even more seriously by grandparents than by donors. They don't care whether the children were conceived within a marriage, in a test tube, or in the backseat of a car—they are still their *grandchildren*.

Ryan explains the connection he has with his donor and his donor grandparents:

> **KNOWING MY DONOR HAS BEEN** *a fascinating experience. Our relationship has changed very little since we first met; I had my questions and he was happy to answer them. We keep in touch and see each other from time to time, but I certainly don't think of him as my "father" nor does he think of me as his "son." We're merely friends who happen to share a very strong genetic connection. On the other hand, the relationship that I built with my donor grandparents is much stronger, mainly due to the fact that we lived in close geographic proximity for a while. What has evolved over the time that I've known them looks very close to a traditional grandparent/grandchild relationship, albeit one that started much later than most. They truly feel like part of my family, and I'm grateful for the opportunity to know them.*

Creating connections with other family members of the donor typically only happens with the donor's support. But even if the donor is entirely uninterested in meeting donor offspring, other family members may provide medical updates or even pursue ongoing relationships. Regardless of the donor's support, you may want to carefully reach out to the donor's parents, siblings, and children, letting them know about your interest in staying in touch. As you explore these links, you can use the techniques we've discussed in earlier chapters. While connections with other members of your donor's family are not a complete substitute for the lack of relationship with a donor, they can still be filled with warmth and insight.

Donors Integrating Offspring and Their Families into Their Current Lives

"A man is a sperm donor for only a short time; after that he becomes a man with children in someone else's family."[5]

Although some donors provide sperm or eggs with the knowledge and acceptance of their partners, many donate while in college or graduate school, before they have established lifelong relationships. At that point, many do not consider their donation's long-term consequences for their own futures and the families they haven't yet created. Later in life, when they learn about their offspring, they're not necessarily certain about what kind of ongoing relationship they want or about how to get there. Howard says, "Two months ago, my donor daughter contacted me through the DSR. I toil over how to maintain boundaries regarding attachments and expectations, while providing limitless information and candor, and getting to know this wonderful, genetically related young person." Howard speaks for many others—donors, parents, and offspring—in seeking to balance the need to develop healthy boundaries and keep expectations in check while also allowing for vulnerability and emotions.

As donors move toward creating their own families, we encourage them to tell their partners early in their relationships about the possibility of offspring. Developing a comfortable balance takes time and patience. Your partner's support can help you work through these issues. The earlier your partner and children know about the possibility of donor offspring, the more accepting they are likely to be if you decide to establish ongoing bonds with your donor offspring. They will feel less worried and threatened if they know that they are part of the decision-making process and can be involved in these new relationships.

That was certainly true for Evan, who has fostered a close relationship between his family and the family of one of his donor offspring:

> **I TOLD MY WIFE SHORTLY AFTER** *we started dating that I had been a donor, so she was very supportive of me when I signed up on the DSR. My wife, daughter, and I have all become part of the extended family of my donor-conceived daughter. We are lucky that they live close enough to get together semi-regularly. The girls (theirs is ten, mine is twelve) have known each other half of their lives and refer to themselves as sisters. I couldn't be happier with how things have turned out for us.*

Some donors wait until their children are older to let them know about the possibility (or reality) of half siblings, and this delay need not turn out badly. George didn't tell his two sons that he was a donor until after he had joined the DSR and had already made contact with several offspring.

> **MY WIFE HAS KNOWN ALL ALONG** *and approved of my donations with the caveat that she did not want to meet or know anything about any of my donor offspring (she is a physician, so she knew what the donations would lead to!). Because of that, I never told my sons; I didn't want to get into a fight with my wife in case my sons felt differently about contact. I realized that I could no longer live by lying, so I told my wife that I needed to tell our children. I broke the news to my boys one evening at a sushi bar by showing them a bunch of pictures of their half siblings, and asking them to guess who they were. The reaction was basically, "Huh?????" Really???" Then in typical fashion it shifted to "So what, and why did you choose to tell us this in such a stupid way?" It is now about two years later, and*

both of them are now "Facebook friends" with a bunch of their "cous-
lings." It turns out that they have many overlapping interests and
they are eager to meet someday.

Although George's sons and Evan's daughter accepted their new family members, other children of donors worry that their new half siblings might want too much of their parent's attention and may be jealous of this new relationship. Your spouse may wonder how you'll find time to spend with new children. It is often hard to see how new half siblings will fit into the family plan. One sperm donor described his wife's reaction this way: "She is supportive of me with respect to the one family I have met, but is extremely concerned about long-term implications of establishing/ maintaining contact with the multitudes of donor kids." Another explained that his wife was "open to the contact, but she does not completely understand. She has concerns that my desire to contact or meet my offspring is a sign that they (my wife and my daughter) are not enough."

In each of these situations, the donor must reassure his current family of his love and commitment to them, explaining how the donor-conceived family members do not threaten his existing relationships. He can learn to prioritize his time commitments. He can involve both families in joint activities, so that he builds double sets of stronger relationships. But he must also be entirely honest, discussing with his spouse his practical and emotional expectations for his new connections. Encouraging family members to read about successful connections on the DSR might be helpful.

Some partners and children will overcome their reluctance to connect if you help them consider the ways new kinship bonds might enrich your family life. Establishing customs, dynamics, and values might initially seem daunting but can instead become exhilarating; ultimately, you will learn more not only about your new family but also about your established one—and yourself. Neal, who has known his donor daughter for four years, tells us about his experience:

> "**FINDING CHRISTIE WAS CERTAINLY** a life-changing experience. Becoming a father overnight to a twelve-year-old was frankly terrifying. Usually parents get a few years of trial and error before the kid remembers anything. Christie probably still remembers the day we met like it was yesterday, as do I. Becoming her father was a growing experience for me, and I credit her with teaching me how to be a father."

Both Christie and her mom have appreciated Neal's involvement in their lives. We listened to donor Todd tell Oprah in 2008 how he has blended his donor kids and their moms with the children from his former marriage to create one large extended family. They take yearly vacations together, sometimes even staying in the same house.

A donor named Jeremy explains:

> **MY (DONOR) DAUGHTER GREW UP** without any father in her house and always knew she was donor-conceived. I learned of my daughter's existence and got into contact with her nearly one year ago, when she was nineteen. I am now actively involved in her life, and we communicate almost daily. My daughter wishes, and I wish too, that we had known each other since she was a baby. I think the key here is that all parties concerned be on the same page. We are fortunate that all concerned are very happy that we are in each other's lives. That includes my daughter's mother and my wife. (My wife has "adopted" my daughter as hers too, and all are thrilled, especially when my wife takes her clothes shopping!) Trouble only occurs when people aren't on the same page.

As Jeremy points out, everyone needs to be explicit about what they want—and what they are able to give. (He indicated quite clearly that he would prefer not to take his daughter shopping!) The actions of his donor family played a critical role in fostering this warmth. And luckily for Jeremy, his wife shared his welcoming attitude, making the situation easier for all involved.

There are many other families where the recipients and the donor's partner have become very close. Katie, a high school junior, and her mom moved across the state to be closer to Katie's newfound biological father, his wife, and their baby boy. Katie embraced her new half brother, and her mom became his full-time babysitter. Because Katie, her mom, the biological father, and his wife all wanted this close connection, the situation has worked out very well.

When donors connect with several offspring, the relationships can vary. Tim, who calls himself both "a donor and a dad," has let each of his offspring define the relationship. He explains:

I'VE MET SEVEN OF MY *biological children and have had every experience along the spectrum—from the son who called me Dad from the first time we spoke on the phone to the one who still calls me by my first name. I don't feel hurt or bothered because this is not about me. I joined the DSR with my own very selfish goal of getting to meet some of the kids I helped to create, but my perspective has really evolved over the past few years. Now I realize I am here to give at least as much as I get.*

I cannot pretend to be their dad in the sense of a caretaking parent who is there for them day in and day out, but the biological reality is that I am their genetic father. How much or how little that connection means is entirely up to each child. Their own concepts on the subject may also change over time. I feel like my role here is

to make myself available to those children who would like to avail
themselves of my availability.

Tim's sensitivity and willingness to react to each child as the child's needs dictate and to allow the relationships to be fluid have made for some very happy kids and moms. The key is his ability to focus on his offspring and respond to what they need rather than imposing his own expectations and hopes for the relationships.

These stories of ongoing success all feature continued communication. Relationships of any sort tend to break up when communication breaks down. Clearly expressing your needs and desires, and listening carefully to everyone—including, crucially, your own inner voice—are essential for building successful ongoing relationships.

Integrating These New Connections into Your Identity

Identity formation and the establishment of self-esteem, central tasks of childhood and adolescence, can be profoundly affected by doubts and mystery about one's origins. Having some of these doubts and mysteries suddenly resolved can be life-changing for each member of the donor family. The once unknown side of yourself is now known, and you need to integrate it into your identity. If you are a parent, you will be adjusting your images of your child based on this new knowledge; if you are a donor-conceived person, then you will arrive at a more complete understanding of yourself.

Until the summer of 2005, when Ryan was fifteen, Wendy was Ryan's *only* parent: she felt that he was 100 percent *her* child. Even so, with every birthday candle he blew out, he wished to meet his biological father (except the year he turned six, when he wished for Free Willy to live in the reservoir near his home). Eventually Ryan was lucky enough to connect with his donor and his donor's parents, and then to meet several half siblings. As Ryan explored the other half of his heritage and ancestry, Wendy came to understand him even better, now knowing the source of some of his traits and talents. It was thrilling for her to watch her son fill in missing pieces and redefine himself.

Ryan understands himself more deeply now too. He explains:

> **WHILE I ALWAYS FELT SECURE** *in my own identity as a result of my upbringing, it was of great interest to me to find the donor (and half siblings who shared my "unknown" DNA) to better understand the "ingredients" that led me to who I am today. Having had the opportunity to have those questions answered has greatly enriched my sense of self and has given me greater insight into my own interests, ambitions, personality, struggles, and ultimately who I am as a person.*

For example, Wendy's side of the family is more extroverted, openly expressing their thoughts and emotions. The donor's side of the family is a bit more reserved. Ryan has aspects of both. Ryan clearly got the "engineering" gene from his donor (they both have the same graduate degree). They were both towheads as children; they share many of the same facial features, and have very similar laughs. Ryan now has an explanation for where he came from, allowing him more certainty as he incorporates these new pieces into his identity and adult self.

While some of Ryan's half siblings have shown curiosity about their biological father and have met him, others don't have the same level of interest. For some, connecting with half siblings, rather than the donor, is an easier way of integrating this newly known side of themselves into their own sense of self. It is often less stressful to bond with peers than with another parent-type figure, who may or may not have expectations about them (and vice versa). In fact, many offspring in two-parent families focus only on finding half siblings because of their fears of hurting one or both of their parents. Learning about and maintaining boundaries can be tricky for donor offspring who are trying to discover more about themselves while also trying to keep all the adults around them happy.

So much of getting to know new family members is fun. Something as simple as noticing whether they laugh or walk or make hand gestures the way you do can be delightful, and you may ascribe many behaviors to your genes. We can discover much when we see half siblings from different parents and the same donor. Stacy, a twenty-four-year-old woman, could trace parts of her appearance and personality to her mother's side of the family but always wondered about the other half.

> **FINDING MY HALF BROTHER** *on the DSR a few years ago helped me immensely because I could see myself in him, and thus see glimpses of what our donor had passed on to us. I guess my favorite analogy to use is that we are all puzzles made up of various pieces that have been given to us by our ancestors, maternal and paternal. Knowing my brother filled in more of my puzzle, enough so that if we never find our donor, we'll still be left with a pretty clear picture of what we had gotten from him.*

"Nature" also makes itself felt in our health, so part of getting to know the donor and half siblings is learning about shared medical conditions or potential health issues. Many donor-sibling groups have connected only to realize that the children are all on the autism spectrum or suffer from various forms of attention deficit/hyperactivity disorder (ADHD), hearing disorders, asthma, and other serious medical problems that seem to stem from their donor's genes. As you learn more, these shared health issues can encourage closeness among families as they support one another by comparing notes, remedies, and diagnostic and testing information.

While genes do have important implications for our behaviors, our health, and even how we understand ourselves, a particular genetic heritage only shows the possibility for certain outcomes but doesn't necessarily control them. Nature isn't everything. As science writer Matt Ridley points out, "Nature plays a role in determining personality, intelligence and health—genes matter. . . . But nature does not prevail over nurture; they do not compete; they are not rivals; it is not nature vs. nurture at all."[6] Birth order, teachers, community, parents, other family members, circumstances, and chance—as well as genes—all contribute to who we are, so it's impossible to say which of our habits and quirks are imprinted in our DNA.

Consequently, meeting genetic relatives won't answer all questions about personality and health, and it is important not to ascribe every trait to genetics either before or after you meet members of your donor family. As numerous studies of twins remind us, you have become who you are not just because of your genes but also because of who raised you, how you were raised, your community, and a host of other influences. For all children, including those born from egg donation, besides getting one half of their DNA from their genetic parents, epigenetic changes (heritable alterations in gene expression caused by mechanisms other than changes in DNA sequence) that occurred while their mom was carrying them, and even afterward, will also affect the people that they become. As you get to know one another, you will undoubtedly be comparing how you are similar and how you are different from one another, even though you share one half of your genes.

chapter eleven

Families Moving Forward

Call it a clan, call it a network, call it a tribe,
call it a family: Whatever you call it,
whoever you are, you need one.

· JANE HOWARD ·

In reaching out and getting to know members of your donor family, you've been open and honest about who you are, what you expect from them, and what they can expect from you. We hope these connections have given you enormous relief and joy. But as you develop new bonds, you may be encountering new challenges and, perhaps, frustrations. People expect genetic relatives to be similar, which can make it more difficult to cope when they turn out to have different approaches to these new relationships (or when they decide to withdraw entirely). While you now have many ideas about how to maintain your relationships, this chapter looks at some of the occasional frustrations donor families might encounter. It gives you effective tools for managing the most common "sticky situations" that arise after communication has been established.

Dealing with Different Expectations

When other families have different expectations for your ongoing relationship, the path forward isn't always clear. An easygoing, understanding attitude is one of the keys to successful donor-family relationships. Without allowing your own enthusiasm to flag, you must accept that not everyone is interested in making a half-sibling relative their new BFF or getting together with other parents for summer vacations.

Phyllis faced a dilemma in managing differing levels of interest. During her five years of membership on the DSR, she had connected with eight of her son's half siblings, and she was successfully navigating people's differing expectations.

SOME OF US GET TOGETHER *regularly; others of us maintain e-mail contact and have met once or twice. I started a Yahoo! Group for us to facilitate contact within the group, and we have created a really strong community together. But then, a new person, Cindy, contacted us this week with two children from the same donor. She is interested in joining our group. She made the following statements: "I don't believe my guys, who are three and five, are actual 'siblings' with all the matches. But I do think it's important to establish contact for them if they're ever interested to meet any of them or for health info. I'm not into meet-ups and gatherings, and I'd like to introduce myself and swap basic info without establishing a familial relationship." I am not sure that she is an appropriate addition to our group, as it doesn't sound like she is willing to share much info.*

How do we navigate this new relationship? Should we let her join the group even though it doesn't sound like she's willing to partici-pate (i.e., share photos, stories, even e-mail)? Should we just provide her with personal e-mail addresses so she can individually contact our other sib families?

Deciding how to manage ongoing relationships within donor-sibling groups can be a delicate process. You must balance everyone's needs for contact and privacy and develop processes for handling contacts. Cindy is clearly just beginning to think through what it means to have found half-sibling families and to join a group. Phyllis needs to determine the level of contact with which she and the other group members feel comfortable. At this point, Cindy's particular interests and relationship preferences are not aligned with those of other group members. Given how young her children are, Cindy will be setting the terms (at least in the short term) for how they relate to their half siblings.

Recognize that, while Cindy might want to maintain distance from the half-sibling group, she is reaching out and so does want *some* form of contact. Her tentativeness might feel like a rejection of the group culture, but the group members should consider the possibility that she is just going slowly, taking her first steps toward openness about donor conception.

In situations like this one, look for a compromise that, in the words of negotiation experts Roger Fisher and William Ury, "expands the pie" by developing different options.[1] Resist making the situation all (join!) or nothing (no contact!). For Cindy, Phyllis's suggestion of providing e-mail addresses without joining the group might satisfy the needs of all in-volved. At this point, private e-mail correspondence with one family at a time might be the best fit for her. Moreover, a gentle approach can in-crease Cindy's level of comfort. As she gets further information and begins to communicate with group members, she may find a sense of community and support with the other parents, whose children probably share many traits with her sons. And even if she herself never decides to join the group, as her children grow and possibly begin to express their own curiosity and interest in knowing about their half siblings, she may start to see the possible benefits of closer relationships to expand their family circle.

Some people are simply not joiners, and group members need to remain open to staying in touch with those who share a donor but want to remain outside of the group.

Privacy vs. Secrecy

As you make each new contact and exchange information, how much do you tell others about yourself or your children? When you learn something about a member of your donor family, how do you know what is okay to tell members of your own family, your donor, or the families of other half siblings? Is it okay for families in your half-sibling DSR or Yahoo! Group to write about the group's members on their own personal blogs or on other Web sites? What if you learn medical information about your child, like a new diagnosis of ADHD or bipolar disorder, for instance, that would help other families, especially those thinking of using your donor, but that you want to keep private? What if a new family, or the donor, contacts you privately through the DSR, requesting that you keep their information confidential, so you can't let others know about this new match? How might withholding this information affect your relationships with the other families? How do you respect others' privacy while taking a stand against secrecy in the donor conception world? Even if you have not yet confronted them in reality, you should begin to consider these issues of ethics and trust.

First, you need to decide how much you are willing to share with the group about yourself, and then think about how what you say will affect other members of your family. This can involve some self-censorship to protect those around you. Betty faced precisely this issue: she told her son when he was a teenager that he was donor-conceived, and he was angry that she hadn't told him sooner. Uncertain of how to respond, she posted on the DSR's Yahoo! Group for advice on how to handle his reaction, acknowledging that she felt guilty for having kept the secret for so long. She then became worried that he might become even more upset if he learned that she had, in any way, publicized his feelings. Shortly thereafter, she added a second posting: "How can I admit to my son that I wrote to this group about his struggles? He doesn't like it when I share his personal business. Do any of you have wise counsel on how to raise this with him?" Betty clearly appreciated the importance of learning from others who had already been through the same situation and of using their advice to help both her son and her, but her second posting also shows that she didn't fully consider how posting publicly about her son's private feelings might affect him. After carefully reading about how others had handled this situation, Betty took responsibility for her requests for guidance and explained to her son why it had been so important to her to reach out to others who had lived through comparable experiences.

Our advice to Betty for her next post is that she focus solely on her own feelings and emotions, looking for help on how to disentangle her guilt from her response to her son. This allows her son to decide for himself whether he wants to reach out to other donor-conceived people who didn't grow up knowing about their origins. So, for example, she might write: "I'm struggling with how to handle my own feelings of guilt that I didn't disclose to my son earlier without letting it infect my relationship with him" or "I'm looking for advice from other parents who have waited to disclose and how to handle family dynamics."

Second, be prepared for others to ask you not to share certain confidences—the identity of the donor, the existence of other unknown donor offspring, the diagnosis of a serious medical condition, one parent's dislike of the donor, or another parent's discomfort with contact. Your child, your spouse, or your parents may ask you not to talk about donor conception in public. How you handle this information depends on how important disclosing might turn out to be. One parent's feelings about another, for example, are rarely appropriate for public airing, so there's no need to worry about keeping that between the two of you. Even if the other parent withdraws from contact, let that parent do the explaining. The challenge is what to do when there are circumstances in which keeping a secret could cause harm to others, such as when you've learned about an urgent medical issue.

Particularly with medical issues, think beyond your own privacy concerns and those of the person who has confided in you. Consider how withholding this information might affect preventive or diagnostic treatment of other children. If you decide other families must know, first encourage the person who told you to inform everyone who needs to know. Explain the importance of sharing, discussing how it could help others take proactive or protective actions. You can also support your source in deciding how to convey the information. If your source cannot be convinced of the importance of revelation, you may feel morally and ethically required to disclose it anyway. In this case, you can try to craft your disclosure in a way that does not include identifying details but that adequately warns people and advises them to seek testing and to contact their sperm bank or egg clinic. In addition to notifying the other families, urgent medical information should be reported to sperm banks, egg agencies, and fertility clinics.

If someone begins a conversation by asking you never to tell anyone what you are about to hear, then you might ask her to stop before she even begins. Explain that you are committed to a policy of openness. If she continues, or if she doesn't try to swear you to secrecy until after she's given you the information, you'll need to figure out what to do based on what you've just heard. Your loyalties can certainly feel divided; the other person may have desperately needed advice on a difficult situation. If you belong to a group, you can try to head off this situation with certain ground rules: members will not withhold important information from one another, and they will not release information, identifying or not, outside of the group. What is said in the group remains in the group. If members don't know whether they can share certain information outside the group, they will check before sharing it.

What to Do When Someone Wants to End Contact

After initial contact, one party may decide to withdraw, not wanting to remain in touch. Parents who connect before telling their children can get cold feet about continuing; they can become uncomfortable about keeping this type of secret. Sometimes parents connect and discover that they don't like one another, or families find that they don't have anything in common other than the donor, or the half siblings just don't bond at all. It is important to acknowledge that not all donor family connections will work out and that this happens for a variety of reasons. If you are the one making the decision not to continue, think through the consequences and let others know of your plans. You can do so in a way that doesn't hurt the feelings of other group members, but that still makes your intent clear; otherwise, you risk harming them and could make it impossible to establish future relationships.

Here's what happened to Sarah and Brian:

MY SON, BRIAN (NOW NINETEEN), *found out he had a sister sib several years ago (thanks to the DSR). The mom, Lauren, contacted me but told me her daughter didn't know she was donor-conceived. She sent photos and lots of info. We were all excited. Then she abruptly ended contact, with no explanation, and never responded to any further e-mails. I assume her husband either found out, or she told him and there was an ultimatum. It was still exciting to see how much my son looked and acted like his half sis (who is one year younger), but Brian felt really burned.*

While Lauren may have had good reasons to protect herself, she didn't understand that reaching out means taking responsibility for how you affect others. Once you connect, you need to recognize that you do assume obligations to others. This doesn't mean you must continue all relationships forever, but it does mean that you need to think through the consequences of your actions and how they may impact others.

Ryan and Wendy dealt with a similar situation, when the mother of two of Ryan's half siblings contacted them after seeing Ryan on *Oprah* in 2003. Even though Ryan had not mentioned his sperm bank or donor number, this woman said that she *knew*, from just looking at his face on her television screen, that he was the half brother to her children. She explained that when she saw Ryan's face, her "world turned upside down." Until then, she had not given much thought to the possibility of half siblings. After establishing initial contact, she abruptly pulled back, explaining that she and her husband had not told their children about their origins and had no plans to do so. Ryan was devastated.

Wendy was shaken and hurt. But mostly, her heart ached for her son. He had waited so long for a connection, and it arrived, only to be immediately pulled out from under him. Wendy had many long conversations with Ryan about why some parents don't tell their children, and she encouraged Ryan to talk through his frustration and sadness at knowing that he might never have the opportunity to know these half siblings. They worked through Ryan's confusion and anger toward the parents. Ryan's heart also ached for these half siblings of his, thinking that they might never learn the truth about their origins and the rest of their genetic family. As Ryan has connected with other half siblings, he has told them about the existence of other half siblings without revealing any details. Nonetheless, everyone wonders, and worries, about this other family: What will happen if and when the children find out that they are donor-conceived? How will they feel when they learn that they have half siblings with whom they could have grown up knowing?

Parents who end contact while their children are younger should think carefully about the future consequences. Your children may be upset one day when they find out what you have done. If you do end contact, you should be careful to be as gentle as possible in order to leave the door open for your children to connect with their half siblings if and when they desire. Even if you don't want to be in ongoing communication, we recommend maintaining an account on the DSR so that you will be informed about new families and medical information.

If you are a donor-conceived person, you may not pursue contact if, for example, you hear from half siblings at a time when you simply cannot handle new contacts. Maybe you have recently started a new job, are planning a wedding, have recently entered college, or are studying for exams. Whatever your life situation, you need to be honest, explaining that you cannot connect right now but that you want to leave open the possibility of doing so in the future.

If you are the seeker trying to get through to an otherwise occupied half sibling, do not take this withdrawal personally. Make sure your match knows that you will be available if and when she changes her mind. It's okay, and important, to be honest about your disappointment, but don't burn any bridges by venting.

Sometimes it is donors who retreat after establishing contact with families. Jacki explains:

> **"OUR DONOR SEEMS TO HAVE GONE** *underground after being contacted. In our first message, he really wanted to meet, but then, after a few more families contacted him, he stopped responding to my e-mails. Jeez . . . forty-six kids is a lot of kids. How could the sperm bank do this to him and to us?"*

Although she's incredibly disappointed, Jacki clearly has no choice but to accept her donor's actions. She might send him one more message, letting him know that although she will not initiate further communication, she will remain open to further contact, and that she requests that he update her about any significant medical issues. She could also offer to coordinate any further messages so that he is not overwhelmed by contact from so many different families. (Potential reasons for her anger at the sperm bank is another issue, one we'll get to in Chapter 12.)

As we've emphasized, when you first communicate with your donor, you should establish clear boundaries so that everyone understands the parameters of this new relationship. It is as important to let the donor know what you *are not* looking for as it is to explain your hopes for future communication. Make clear that the ball is in his court. While some donors are happy to share their Facebook pages, others might feel that offspring families should not interfere with their personal lives. Donors with many offspring, like Jacki's, will certainly struggle more with these issues, so they need to be straightforward with each and every family about their privacy needs.

If someone ends contact, don't give up. Brian's mother, Sarah, tells us what happened after that first unsuccessful connection:

WHEN WE FOUND OUT ABOUT *another sister (who is one year older than he is), Brian wasn't very interested. He'd already been burned and didn't want to get his hopes up. I actually e-mailed with the young woman for about a year before my son e-mailed her. I encouraged him to contact her because she seemed to be a good person, and I thought they had a lot in common. She has two moms, and a sister with a different donor-dad, so her family is fine with contact and talking about donor conception. They haven't met in person, but he and his donor sis are Facebook friends and talk on the phone fairly often. They plan to meet sometime this year (she's several states away). I am really glad for my son to have this special friend.*

Managing Many: Ten, Fifty, or More Matches

One mom in a large group tells us:

IN THIS DAY AND AGE, *family is what you make it. Our kids have an advantage by having a large family. There are more people to love your child. Most of the families in our group are open. When I first came to the DSR in 2005, there were five or six families on the DSR at that time. My partner wasn't too excited, but we ultimately decided that we wanted to reach out. At first, we formed a Yahoo! Group with six or seven families, and, by the end of the first year, we had grown to fifteen families. We grew slowly for a few years, and then another thirty families joined in one year. We're now at more than 160 kids.*

At our first reunion, when we had fifteen kids together at a restaurant, the waitress asked us, "Is this a family reunion?" All of the kids resemble each other.

We have seventeen children within driving distance of my house. Thirty-five of us met at Disney a few years ago. When my kids were little, as they met new half siblings, they became "new friends" and had an instant bond with every child they've met. Before meeting, they ask questions like, "Do they play hockey?" and "Who else has curly hair?"

We are all good support for one another, and we share medical information. A few of our children have autism, and at least one has diabetes. We know that our support was invaluable when one mother talked to us about the possibility of an organ transplant.

Some groups, like this one, expand gracefully, incorporating new members as they come. But, of course, this isn't always true, and the sheer size of the group can be intimidating. How do you, as a parent, establish and maintain contact with the fifty match families you see posted on the DSR? How do you, as a donor, come to terms with the fact that your sperm has helped to create thirty, fifty, or even more than a hundred children? As a donor-conceived person, how do you get to know eighteen half siblings? Managing longer-term relationships with so many people, balancing all those competing personalities and time commitments, can feel overwhelming.

For some donors, establishing relationships with five or even ten offspring can be exciting. By contrast, after connecting with a few offspring, some donors can feel overwhelmed, refuse additional contact requests, and even discontinue budding relationships. After a period of contemplation and adjustment, they may or may not decide to reverse this understandable withdrawal. If they feel pressure from parents or offspring, they are more likely to shut down completely and refuse to maintain established contacts. Lots of patience, from everyone, is critical.

Very large groups can present challenges for parents as well as for donors. One mom who is a part of a donor-sibling Yahoo! Group approaching two hundred people told us,

> **A LOT OF THE MOMS** are worried that people will find out that they used this donor with so many kids. They don't want their children to become some type of circus sideshow. I would like my daughter to meet these kids when she is old enough to understand. I stay in touch for that reason. I find it interesting to see the pictures and hear what the kids are doing. There are a lot of similarities in interests and abilities. There are also a lot of physical similarities.

She believed that she had also identified her donor but received a mixed response from the others in her group when she disclosed this information:

> **I POSTED THAT I WAS** pretty sure that I had found our donor. When my daughter was napping I did a Google search. I put about five things in and a Web site from this man's work popped up, complete with picture. The man looked just like my daughter. I mean, stunning resemblance. I posted the link to our Yahoo! Group. A lot of people were thrilled to see that he is happy and healthy. They were saying how much he looked like their kids. Others were mad. They said they never wanted to know who he was or see a picture of him. It was odd to me. A lot of these women could not even fathom that a real person was partially responsible for creating their child. They somehow felt very threatened by this.

While a delicate touch is always needed, this is particularly true in large groups that grow quickly, when you don't know everyone and you may not each share the same expectations. It is harder and can take longer to establish the same shared levels of trust as in a smaller group. Remember that not everyone will share your curiosity, and don't assume that everyone has the same goals and interests. This mom could have, instead, shared her excitement about finding the man she believes is the donor but suggested that other group members e-mail her for more information and the link.

When you sense any hesitation from others—donors, half siblings, or parents—take a close look at the type, frequency, and length of your communications. For example, while electronic communication is essential for establishing initial contact and is often necessary for maintaining contact within large groups, it can sometimes be difficult to convey complexity and nuance through e-mail messages alone. As best-selling author Daniel Goleman, the author of *Emotional Intelligence*, points out, "In contrast to a phone call or talking in person, email is emotionally lean."[2] Consequently, you want to be careful to express your emotions as fully as you can in an e-mail message. (Phone calls to all 150 group members would be very difficult!)

Being mindful in your communications and getting to know one family at a time can make large family dynamics manageable. This is where the DSR's messaging system, a Yahoo! or Gmail Group page, or a Facebook page can be helpful. After joining, you can observe and read about the other families before doing anything else. Then you can choose whether to reach out to the families that live closest to you, or with whom you feel that you might have the most in common, to arrange phone calls and eventually set up meetings.

WE ARE PART OF *a donor-sibling group that as of next month (there are twins on the way) will number twenty-nine children. When we started, there were just three families, so it was easy to get to know one another. We just returned from our fourth annual gathering where eleven donor siblings and their parents attended. I posted* *a Success Story on the DSR a couple of years ago when a large group of us first met. I am happy to report that since that time our friendships and true affection for each other's children have continued to grow. We've moved from sharing pictures and comparing traits among our kids to providing support and advice to each other, as the kids get older, parenting challenges get more complex, and our respective life circumstances change.*

Meeting up first with smaller groups of half-sibling families helps you start the process of getting to know everyone. You might also decide that, even though you'll remain in an Internet group, you won't reach out individually to each of the families. Since most large groups are spread out across the country, and even across oceans, it is doubtful that everyone will be able to attend the same meeting. Instead, it's more likely that meetings will be local or organized around vacations or family events. The size of your meetings depends on individuals' comfort level as well as on money, jobs, and school schedules.

Inevitably, half siblings find that they are closer to some members of their group than others; the only concern is making sure that no one feels excluded. Larger groups may experience other tensions. Most groups operate by consensus, in an egalitarian manner, but one parent may try to exert too much control. Secrecy and privacy can also be hot-button issues with so many individual expectations in play. As in any community, it will be hard to satisfy everyone's needs all the time. A simple set of rules for managing large groups starts with being open to new members and making sure that everyone understands the basic ground rules concerning information sharing and privacy.

Cyndi noted that large groups can pose problems when it comes to managing connections with other families, but they can also raise psychological and emotional concerns for donor offspring, who now have to cope with dozens of new half siblings.

> **WE HAVE A LARGE DONOR** *sibling group—fifty-five kids that we know of. We've been fortunate to connect with each other on the DSR and have established an annual gathering so that some of the kids can get to know each other. While it is something I've grown to appreciate, it is also something I wasn't prepared for. There is definitely benefit for my kids to know their donor siblings. I know that research indicates that this is important. However, it's been hard to know how the sheer numbers of siblings will affect my kids. There are parenting implications when other families' decisions and lives intersect with your own in this unusual way. "Interesting" is definitely one way to describe our cross-pollinated family!*

While Cyndi is absolutely right about the importance of connecting, parents are critical in helping their children adjust to being members of a large group. The strategies of connecting slowly and carefully work just as well for offspring as for parents and donors.

Larger groups may experience other tensions that they'll need to take the time to work through. Just as in any community, it can be challenging to try to satisfy everyone's needs all the time. No matter how hard you try, you can't make everyone happy all of the time, but you can certainly strive to make most of the people happy most of the time.

Getting to Know You

As you work to find your own comfort zone while respecting the needs of an evolving cast of stranger-relatives, know that you are not alone. So

many of us are creating and learning about similarly unfolding relationships right alongside you. As we watch half siblings become aunts and
uncles to each other's children, and donors become grandparents to their
offspring's children, we'll continue to widen our definition of family.
We'll better understand how these families evolve over the long term. But
for now, we are all just beginning to experience and define these new
connections.

chapter twelve

Challenges within the Industry and the Need for Reform

If you want to truly understand something,
try to change it.

· KURT LEWIN ·

As we learn more about the challenges and possibilities of donor families, we need to step back and look carefully at the reproductive medicine industry in the United States. It could play a significant role in creating connections and assisting families in understanding more about the needs and interests of everyone involved in donor conception—children, parents, and donors. But it has primarily focused on helping to achieve pregnancy and profiting from the sale of eggs and sperm. We advocate various reforms from both within and outside of the fertility industry to make the whole donor conception process more humane and more responsive to the needs of the families it has helped create. Our advocacy results from our experience with donor-conceived families and grows out of years of research on these issues. Here is what we are working to change.

1. **COUNSELING:** Require mandatory third-party
counseling for all prospective donors and parents.

> **I DONATED DURING MEDICAL SCHOOL,** *and no one at the sperm*
> *bank talked to me about anything other than whether my sperm were*
> *good enough and how much I would get paid. The ethical and social*
> *implications of donating sperm didn't dawn on me at the time, were*
> *not explained or introduced to me at the time, and only became real*
> *when I began to be contacted by donor children.*

The great majority of surveyed sperm and egg donors say that they were not adequately counseled about the impact of donating. They need to understand that they are helping to create babies, not consumer products. Donors should know that children might eventually seek connections. Thanks to the Internet and advances in genetic technology, there can no longer be any guarantee of anonymity for donors.

While most donations remain anonymous, some sperm banks, clinics, and agencies offer donors the choice to be "open" donors, which allows any children that they help to produce to contact them when the children turn eighteen. Indeed, many egg clinics/agencies (no sperm banks yet) are now counseling egg donors and recipient families to connect on the DSR during pregnancy or right after the child is born. This allows the families to be in touch with one another, anonymously if desired, right from the get-go. (It also alleviates the responsibility of the clinic/agency to act as a middleman.) These forward-thinking clinics and agencies are setting a trend that not only allows for adequate counseling on the importance of these family connections but also offers a safe way to establish these con-nections.

Sperm banks, egg agencies, and clinics should require all prospective donors to receive independent counseling or participate in a group educational session. The counseling would be based on the most recent research on offspring, parents, and donors, and it should cover: (a) the legal, medical, moral, and mental health implications of donating gametes for donors, recipients, and offspring; and (b) the possibility of future contact. Donors should be aware of how many children could result from their donations.

Donors also need to understand the gravity of this decision to donate, including learning about the yearnings of so many donor-conceived people to know about their heritage, ancestry, and medical backgrounds. While counseling or an educational session might result in a slight cost increase, the long-term impact justifies this additional expense.

There is no standard contract that all sperm banks, egg agencies, and clinics use when they are recruiting donors, and practices vary. At the least, donors should: (a) sign informed consents that they are aware of the medical and psychological risks and benefits of the donation procedure; and (b) sign contracts indicating they are aware that they are giving up all legal and financial rights as parents. These documents should be standardized across the industry. To ensure their validity, new laws must enshrine the principle that anonymous donors have no legal rights or obligations to any offspring produced from their gametes. Many donors currently do not make themselves available for contact because they are afraid of possible legal and financial consequences.

Prospective parents should receive appropriate third-party counseling and, like donors, be informed about recent research on donor families to ensure that they appreciate any and all issues related to raising donor offspring, including the importance of telling their children about their origins and the strong possibility of numerous half siblings. Even before they become parents, they need to know about the importance of appreciating and respecting their child's potential curiosities and desires to connect with genetic relatives. They should also understand that their children could already, or may someday, have many half brothers and sisters.

Although the American Society for Reproductive Medicine recommends respect for the rights of donors to be fully informed, the reality is quite different. To ensure uniform implementation of these recommendations concerning counseling and education for both parents and donors, we need national legislation.

2. **MEDICAL TESTING**: Mandate comprehensive medical and genetic testing for donors.

All donors should be required to undergo comprehensive medical and genetic testing. Today, they are tested primarily for sexually transmitted or viral diseases—illnesses such as HIV, hepatitis B and C, syphilis, gonorrhea, and chlamydia. While these tests are necessary, they barely skim the surface of illnesses and disorders that could affect offspring. Currently there are no other nationally mandated and comprehensive testing requirements or regulations. As a result, *some* clinics and sperm banks test *some* donors for *some* diseases. A study by members of the reproductive industry acknowledging these issues noted the enormous variation among facilities, and recommended additional medical and genetic testing for donors.[1] Ninety-three percent of surveyed sperm donors indicated that they would have been open to genetic testing if it had been offered to them.[2]

Recommended Testing for All Donors

Some examples of testing that should be mandatory include: karyotyping, cystic fibrosis, Tay-Sachs, fragile X, hemochromatosis (for HFE mutation), BRCA 1 and 2, celiac disease, polyposis conditions caused by mutations in the APC (adenomatous polyposis coli) gene, hereditary non-polyposis colorectal cancer (HNPCC), glycogen storage diseases such as Fabry disease and Niemann-Pick disease, polycystic disease, Huntington's disease, and melanoma (CDKN2A gene). As genetic testing becomes even more sophisticated, so too should the testing of donor gametes. Kirk Maxey, a former sperm donor who is a physician himself, recommends this required genetic testing:

> **FULL GENOMIC SEQUENCING** *of the entire donor genome at high coverage required, with reporting of each variant known in the Johns Hopkins "Online Mendelian Inheritance in Man (OMIM)" database (approximately twelve thousand genetic illnesses and traits). The sperm bank must report to both the donor and any possible recipient the presence of all known mutations, deletions, duplications, and chromosomal rearrangements, and provide genetic counseling sufficient to enable recipients to use the donor only under the conditions of fully informed consent. Such genetic counseling must also allow the donor to understand his own personal medical and health risks and conditions.*

Moreover, in addition to the genetic testing, all donors need to undergo more thorough physical examinations including organ function, a face-to-face medical history intake, and full psychological screening.

3. **UPDATING MEDICAL HISTORIES:** Require donors (a) to provide a full medical history at the time of donation, and (b) to update their family medical history regularly. This information must then be made available to families who have used the donor's gametes. Families must also update their own medical histories.

When donors sign up today, they fill out a medical information form. This is a snapshot of one day in the life of a healthy young donor that provides limited and unverified information about the donor. Once they've donated, most donors have no further contact with the fertility facility, and they are not required to provide any additional medical information. This means that even if they develop a medical issue (many diseases are late-onset and might not show up until many years later), none of their potentially hundreds of offspring may ever find out about it. We always knew, anecdotally, that most egg and sperm donors were never contacted for updated medical information, but we were surprised to learn, through 2009 DSR research, just how many "most" is: 98 percent of surveyed egg donors and 84 percent of surveyed sperm donors report never having been contacted by their clinics to update health information after donation. Also stunning was the fact that almost one-third (31 percent) of egg donors and one-quarter (23 percent) of sperm donors felt that they, or close family members, had medical issues that would be important for families to know about.

After corresponding with many donor families who have faced medical issues, Dr. Maxey is also quite concerned about industry practice:

> I DID JUST A LITTLE RESEARCH *as to how sperm banks and egg agencies have actually reacted in the past when informed either by a donor or by a physician that there may be genetic defects in their frozen sample vials. We already know that when parents notify the fertility agency, they get a mixture of denial, prevarication, and general indifference. In several documented cases that I found, one in which a donor provided the information and another in which a physician did so, the first response by the bank was to destroy (incinerate) the remaining vials. In both cases, this significantly hampered physicians from pinpointing the source and time of the mutation event. In the case where the physician provided the information, the donor was never found or notified; in the second case, the bank waited for three years and then notified the remaining recipient*

families and offered them counseling. So . . . the record falls far short of anything that might be confused with the ethical practice of medicine.

At the time of donation, donors should report any significant health issues that might affect offspring, ranging from ADHD to genetic heart defects, and that information must be distributed to families. Facilities could be required to conduct their own comprehensive medical histories as well to ensure that the donors have fully reported relevant conditions. When they donate, donors should also sign contracts in which they agree to provide regular medical updates, both annually and when a medically significant event occurs. These medical updates could be filed directly with the clinic or a central data bank, and then made available to all families who are thinking about using, or who have already utilized, that particular donor. Parents who are searching for their "perfect" donor should know as much as is reasonably possible about their donor's health history as well as whether he already has sixty children and how many of them have reported genetic illnesses or other medical problems. Parents and offspring need to be able to share ongoing information about the health of their families, and they should also be *required* to report medically significant events.

4. **IMPROVING RECORD KEEPING:** Track all recipients, donors, and births and safeguard all records in a central data bank indefinitely, with information accessible only to involved families. Limit the number of births from the sperm or eggs of any given donor.

The current, commonly quoted "estimates" of children born in the United States each year from donor gametes—thirty thousand to sixty thousand births per year—are based on an incomplete study published in 1988.[3] The truth is, no one has any idea how many donor children have been born. No one is keeping track.

The federal government attempts to track the success rates of fertility clinics, but clinics are only asked (not required) to report births from donor eggs. Not only is this data incomplete (it does not include sperm donors, who are the majority of gamete providers), but its reliability is questionable. In a paper published in 2013,[4] a study of 108 egg donor parents revealed that more than 40 percent of the surveyed parents were not ever asked to report back about the birth of their child. This record keeping is inaccurate and inadequate, and it becomes even more worrisome with the increasing popularity of egg banking.

The federal government does not require sperm banks to report any data concerning vials sold or the number of children born, although they are required to keep records for a limited period of time on the results of testing for some communicable diseases.[5] No federal law imposes limits on how often, and over what length of time, donors can produce gametes, nor are there limits on the number of different banks or agencies where they can donate. Families are not required to report whether a particular vial of sperm has resulted in a birth.

The government must take a series of steps to improve monitoring and safety. First, it must require better record keeping from the assisted reproductive technology field by mandating that all clinics and sperm banks report on the number of births from each donor. Second, each donor must be assigned a specific tracking number based on a genetic marking test to make sure that donors don't donate at several facilities. Third, the number of offspring per donor should be legally limited. In the United Kingdom, for example, one donor's gametes can be used by no more than ten families. Although there are suggested limits from the US fertility industry of the number of offspring per donor (twenty-five pregnancies from one donor within a given population of eight hundred thousand[6]—in New York City, for example, this would allow for almost three hundred donor-conceived children to be born from the same donor, which is approximately one child per square mile), even these are not binding. Mandated limits would ensure that one donor does not spread diseases to dozens of offspring and would also protect children from the psychological consequences of learning that they are the 150th in a "herd" of other children.

5. **PROMOTE RESEARCH:** Support studies on the long-term consequences of donor conception, particularly on egg donors' health.

Research on the consequence of donor conception for offspring, donors, and their parents is becoming more common, and more research on these issues through both private and public funding is critical. But one group has been neglected: women who have donated eggs. Long-term studies are needed to ascertain oocyte donors' risks of secondary infertility, ovarian hyperstimulation syndrome, and cancer.

6. **END DONOR ANONYMITY.**

> *"I wonder what it would be like had I been conceived in an open system, growing up with information about my natural father, and in due course knowing his name, perhaps even meeting him. I am sure it would have been infinitely preferable to my actual experience of secrecy, followed by the brick wall of protected anonymity. I imagine living with my social father, knowing something about, and anticipating in due course a meeting with, my biological father."*
>
> *—Dani, donor-conceived adult*

Finally, and most radically, we must ban donor anonymity. Our society has not ignored the anguish of infertility. Parents' reproductive rights are, for the most part, given profound respect. But the rights of the donor child have been severely neglected. When other countries have considered children's best interests, they have concluded that anonymity violates the basic human rights of the donor-conceived. Anonymity is now banned in the United Kingdom, the Netherlands, Sweden, Norway, Finland, Switzerland, Austria, New Zealand, and the Australian states of Victoria, New South Wales, and Western Australia.

More than three-quarters of surveyed donor offspring recommended that only known or willing-to-be-known donors should be used. As striking as this is, it fails to take into account the experiences of another group of donor-conceived people who would have benefited from truth and openness: those who have never been told about their origins but who may nevertheless have experienced a lifelong uneasiness as a consequence.

The industry claims to be worried that if anonymity disappears, the supply of donor eggs and sperm will disappear with it. The experiences of other countries, such as the United Kingdom, proves that this is not necessarily true, and innovative research in the United States shows that ending anonymity might drive up prices but should have little impact on the supply.[7] Many donors support this move as well:

> **I WANT ALL MY GENETIC OFFSPRING** to be happy and healthy like my own children. I will always wonder where they are, what they are doing, are they living, learning and experiencing life like my own children and me? I hope that they are bringing the same joy to the lives of all the mothers and dads the same way my life has been enriched by my own children. We are, and will always be, connected. Some of them will become equally as curious as I was someday, and want to know more. I think we owe it to them to let them learn.

As other countries have done, the United States must consider whether a donor's potential interest in remaining anonymous should continue to trump donor-conceived people's rights to know where they come from. This is *not* about parents' rights to reproduce or about limiting parents' right to choose egg or sperm donors. This is about honoring the rights of parents to create new families, respecting the rights of children to know about their origins, and acknowledging the rights of donors to make mutual-consent contact with the children they have helped to create. It is about developing policies that have *everyone's* best interests at heart. And it is about recognizing human connection.

postscript from wendy:
Connecting to
the Future

I n 2005, when my fifteen-year-old son, Ryan, first met his biological father and grandparents, I witnessed a profound change come over him. There was a sense of peace, of wholeness, that had not been there before. Many times over that weekend, Ryan would turn to me, wide-eyed and smiling, almost as if in shock, and say, "I *know* who my donor is." On the plane ride home he told me, "If I never see those people again, I'll be okay. *I know where I come from.*" He considered any continuing relationship to be purely bonus material, adding on to his already remarkable story.

Since then, Ryan has had the opportunity to establish loving relationships with his biological father and grandparents, and also with several of his half siblings. We estimate that there are many more half siblings out there and Ryan and all of his known donor relatives remain open to, and excited about, expanding their family.

For many years, it has been my honor at the Donor Sibling Registry to support and advise people who have become a part of our donor family community. I have walked this path alongside you, sharing the frustrations of waiting, the tears when things go wrong, and the joy when we find new family. Together, we've grieved for the failed connections, faced the unknown, and reveled in the successes. We've explored all of this previously uncharted territory as a community, teaching and learning from each other's experiences.

As more people use donor conception, and as more donor families find each other and establish relationships, we will all learn even more about the possibilities of these previously undefined and unimagined connections. I hope that we've helped you to discover a new appreciation for fundamental values: the sacred responsibility of parenthood, the importance of protecting children's interests, and the inherent worth of kinship bonds. Our stories and collected research illuminate the human desire and capacity for connection, and we hope that we have enlarged your sense of family and the preciousness of life.

acknowledgments

We thank Sonia Allan, Kate Bourne, Susan Frankel, Tony Gambino, McKenzie Gibson, Rosanna Hertz, Ryan Kramer, Kris Probasco, Alexis Rebane, and Ruth Shidlo for reading earlier versions of the book and for their incredibly helpful comments and suggestions. We appreciate the research assistance of Mary Kate Hunter at GW, and the endnote checking expertise of Melinda Dudley. For helping shepherd us through the publishing process, we thank Bridget Wagner Matzie and Todd Shuster at Zachary Shuster Harmsworth, and Marisa Vigilante and Sophia Muthuraj at Gotham & Avery Books. Thanks to Robin Bellinger for her wordsmithing and editorial assistance.

A very special THANK YOU to all the Donor Sibling Registry members who have shared their stories. You are the heart and soul of this book!

notes

Introduction

1. Kiley Armstrong, "Ellis Island Gives Springsteen Heritage Award," *USA Today*, April 22, 2010, http://usatoday30.usatoday.com/life/people/2010-04-22 -springsteen-ellis-island_N.htm.

Chapter 1

1. S. Golombok, V. Jadva, E. Lycett, C. Murray, and F. MacCallum, "Families Created by Gamete Donation: Follow-Up at Age 2," *Human Reproduction* 20, no. 1 (January 2005): 286–93, doi: 10.1093/humrep/deh585.

2. Diane Beeson, Patricia K. Jennings, and Wendy Kramer, "Offspring Searching for Their Sperm Donors: How Family Type Shapes the Process," *Human Reproduction* 26, no. 9 (September 2011): 2415–24, doi: 10.1093/humrep/der202; Neroli Sawyer, Lucy Frith, Eric Blyth, and Wendy Kramer, "A Survey of 1700 Recipients of Donor Sperm: The Views of Women Who Formed Their Families Using Donor Sperm," *RBM Online* (in press).

Chapter 2

1. Elspeth, "Conception, Deception, Identity and Relationships," *Donor Conception Network Journal* 1 (2009): 4.

2. David Lundberg Kenrick, "What Secret Is Your Spouse Keeping from You?: What Secret Are You Keeping from Your Spouse?," *Psychology Today*, May 27,

2010, http://www.psychologytoday.com/blog/the-caveman-goes
-hollywood/201005/what-secret-is-your-spouse-keeping-you.

3. Michael L. Slepian, E. J. Masicampo, Negan R. Toosi, and Nalini Ambady, "The Physical Burdens of Secrecy," *Journal of Experimental Psychology: General* 141 (March 5, 2012): 619–24.

4. Sharon Jayson, "Can You Keep a Secret?," *USA Weekend*, July 29, 2010, http://www.usaweekend.com/article/20100730/HOME03/8010314/Can-you -keep-secret (reporting on Vangelisti's observations).

5. Deborah H. Siegel and Susan Livingston Smith, "Openness in Adoption: From Secrecy and Stigma to Knowledge and Connections," *Evan B. Donaldson Adoption Institute* (March 2012): 23, http://www.adoptioninstitute.org/research/2012_03_ openness.php.

6. Vasanti Jadva, Tabitha Freeman, Wendy Kramer, and Susan Golombok, "The Experiences of Adolescents and Adults Conceived by Sperm Donation: Comparisons by Age of Disclosure and Family Type," *Human Reproduction* 24 (2009): 1915, doi: 10.1093/humrep/dep110.

7. Beeson, Jennings, and Kramer, "Offspring Searching for Their Sperm Donors: How Family Type Shapes the Process," 2415–24, doi: 10.1093/ humrep/der202.

8. Diane Ehrensaft, *Mommies, Daddies, Donors, Surrogates: Answering Tough Questions and Building Strong Families* (New York: Guilford Press, 2005), 162.

9. Ken Daniels, Wayne Gillett, and Victoria Grace, "Parental Information Sharing with Donor Insemination Conceived Offspring: A Follow-Up Study," *Human Reproduction* 24, no. 5 (May 2009): 1104, doi: 10.1093/humrep/den495.

10. Britta Dinsmore, "Disclosure Decisions," *Parents via Egg Donation*, accessed April 24, 2013, http://parentsviaeggdonation.org/disclosure.html.

11. Patricia P. Mahlstedt, Kathleen LaBounty, and William Thomas Kennedy, "The Views of Adult Offspring of Sperm Donation: Essential Feedback for the Development of Ethical Guidelines Within the Practice of Assisted Reproductive Technology in the United States," *Fertility and Sterility* 93, no. 7 (May 1, 2010): 2236.

12. Susan Golombok, Jennifer Readings, Lucy Blake, Polly Casey, Laura Mellish, Alex Marks, and Vasanti Jadva, "Children Conceived by Gamete Donation: Psychological Adjustment and Mother-Child Relationships at Age 7," *Journal of Family Psychology* 25, no. 2 (April 2011): 230–39.

Chapter 3

1. Ellen Sarasohn Glazer and Evelina Weidman Sterling, *Having Your Baby Through Egg Donation* (Indianapolis, IN: Perspectives Press, Inc., 2005), 282.

2. Karey A. Harwood, *The Infertility Treadmill: Feminist Ethics, Personal Choice, and the Use of Reproductive Technologies* (Chapel Hill: University of North Carolina Press, 2007), 138.

3. Eric Blyth, Wendy Kramer, and Jennifer Schneider, "Perspectives, Experiences, and Choices of Parents of Children Conceived Following Oocyte Donation," *Reproductive BioMedicine Online* 26, no. 2 (February 2012): 179–88, doi 10.1016/j.rbmo.2012.10.013.

4. Jenni Colson, "Adoption Scrapbooks Made Easy," *Adoptive Families*, accessed April 23, 2013, http://www.adoptivefamilies.com/articles.php?aid=1131.

5. Sherrie Eldridge, *20 Things Adopted Parents Need to Succeed: Discover the Secrets to Understanding the Unique Needs of Your Adopted Child and Become the Best Parent You Can Be* (New York: Delta, 2009), 60.

6. Sherrie Eldridge, *Twenty Things Adopted Kids Wish Their Adoptive Parents Knew* (New York: Delta, 1999), 102.

7. Kris Probasco, "Third Party Reproduction—Explaining Donor Conception," *Adoptive Families*, accessed April 23, 2013, http://www.adoptivefamilies.com/articles/2315/index.php.

8. Ehrensaft, *Mommies, Daddies, Donors, Surrogates: Answering Tough Questions and Building Strong Families*, 158.

9. Ibid., 159.

Chapter 4

1. Ehrensaft, *Mommies, Daddies, Donors, Surrogates: Answering Tough Questions and Building Strong Families*, 233.

2. "Woman Heads to B.C. in Battle for Biological Data," *Legal Feeds*, February 23, 2012, http://www.canadianlawyermag.com/legalfeeds/date/2012/2/13.html.

3. Olivia Montuschi, "Why Is It That D.C. People Feel So Differently about Their Conception?," *oliviasview*, March 27, 2012, http://oliviasview.wordpress.com/2012/03/27/why-is-it-that-dc-people-feel-so-differently-about-their-conception.

4. Ibid.

5. Elspeth, "Conception, Deception, Identity and Relationships," 2.

6. Rebecca Hamilton. "Open Parents, Closed System," in *Behind Closed Doors: Moving Beyond Secrecy and Shame*, ed. Mikki Morrissette (Minneapolis, MN: Be-Mondo Publishing, 2006), 44.

Chapter 5

1. Olivia Montuschi, "Parenting Donor Conceived Children: Is it Different?," *oliviasview*, May 1, 2012, http://oliviasview.wordpress.com/2012/05/01/1178.

2. Glazer and Sterling, *Having Your Baby Through Egg Donation*, 301.

3. Montuschi, "Parenting Donor Conceived Children: Is it Different?"

4. Glazer and Sterling, *Having Your Baby Through Egg Donation*, 298.

Chapter 6

1. Vasanti Jadva, Tabitha Freeman, Wendy Kramer, and Susan Golombok, "Experiences of Offspring Searching for and Contacting Their Donor Siblings and Donor," *Reproductive BioMedicine Online* 20, no. 4 (April 2010): 523–32.

2. Cheryl Shuler, *Sperm Donor = Dad: A Single Woman's Story of Creating a Family with an Unknown Donor* (Denver, CO: Outskirts Press, 2010), 131.

3. Katrina Clark, "My Father Was an Anonymous Sperm Donor," *Washington Post*, December 17, 2006, http://www.washingtonpost.com/wp-dyn/content/article/2006/12/15/AR2006121501820.html.

4. "Surgeon General's Family Health History Initiative," US Department of Health and Human Services, accessed April 23, 2013, http://hss.gov/familyhistory.

5. Tamsin Eva, "Donor Siblings, and a New Kind of Family," *New York Times*, July 1, 2012, http://parenting.blogs.nytimes.com/2012/07/01/donor-siblings-and-a-new-kind-of-family.

6. Rosanna Hertz, "Turning Strangers into Kin: Half Siblings and Anonymous Donors," in *Who's Watching?: Daily Practices of Surveillance among Contemporary Families*, ed. Margaret K. Nelson and Anita Ilta Garey (Nashville, TN: Vanderbilt University Press, 2009),156, 163.

7. For further discussion, see Naomi R. Cahn, *Test Tube Families: Why the Fertility Market Needs Legal Regulation* (New York: New York University Press, 2009); Naomi R. Cahn, *The New Kinship: Constructing Donor-Conceived Families* (New York: New York University Press, 2013); Susan L. Crockin and Howard W. Jones Jr., *Legal Conceptions: The Evolving Law and Policy of Assisted Reproductive Technologies* (Baltimore, MD: Johns Hopkins University Press, 2009).

8. Jadva, Freeman, Kramer, and Golombok, "Experiences of Offspring Searching for and Contacting their Donor Siblings and Donor."

9. Tom Kelly, "British Scientist 'Fathered 600 Children' by Donating Sperm at His Own Fertility Clinic," *Daily Mail Online*, April 9, 2012, http://www.dailymail.co.uk/health/article-2126761/Bertold-Wiesner-British-scientist-fathered-600-children-donating-sperm-fertility-clinic.html.

Chapter 7

1. "Richard Hatch and the Donor Sibling Registry," *Donor Sibling Registry*, February 8, 2012, https://www.donorsiblingregistry.com/blog/?p=357.

2. Kathleen R. LaBounty, "The Way Life Unfolds," *Child of a Stranger: Conception Through Anonymous Sperm Donation*, December 13, 2008, http://childofastranger .blogspot.com/2008/12/way-life-unfolds.html.

3. "Sperm-Donor Siblings Unite Online: Banks Don't Disclose Medical Information, So Moms Seek Answers Elsewhere," NBCNews.com, August 11, 2006, http:// www.msnbc.msn.com/id/14307725/ns/health-health_care/t/sperm-donor -siblings-unite-online; Rachel Lehmann-Haupt, "Are Sperm Donors Really Anonymous Anymore?: DNA Testing Makes Them Easy to Trace," *Slate.com*, March 1, 2010, http://www.slate.com/articles/double_x/doublex/2010/02/are_ sperm_donors_really_anonymous_anymore.html.

Chapter 8

1. Rosanna Hertz and Jane Mattes, "Donor-Shared Siblings or Genetic Strangers: New Families, Clans, and the Internet," *Journal of Family Issues* 32, no. 9 (September 2011): 1141, doi:10.1177/0192513X11404345.

2. Ibid., 1139.

3. Ibid., 1138.

4. Jean A. S. Strauss, *Birthright: The Guide to Search and Reunion for Adoptees, Birthparents, and Adoptive Parents* (New York: Penguin Books, 1994), 126.

5. Ken Daniels, Wendy Kramer, and Maria Perez-y-Perez, "Semen Donors Who Are Open to Contact with Their Offspring: Issues and Implications for Them and Their Families," *Reproductive BioMedicine Online* 25, no. 7 (December 2012): 670, doi: 10.1016/j.rbmo.2012.09.009.

6. Hertz, "Turning Strangers into Kin: Half Siblings and Anonymous Donors," in *Who's Watching: Daily Practices of Surveillance among Contemporary Families*, 156, 167.

Chapter 9

1. Sherrie Eldridge, *Twenty Life-Transforming Choices Adoptees Need to Make* (Colorado Springs, CO: Piñon Press, 2003), 228.

Chapter 10

1. Jadva, Freeman, Kramer, and Golombok, "Experiences of Offspring Searching for and Contacting Their Donor Siblings and Donor," 523–32.

2. Emily Bazelon, "The Children of Donor X," *O, The Oprah Magazine*, April 2008, http://www.oprah.com/relationships/Autism-Aspergers-and-The-Donor-Sibling -Registry.

3. Rosanna Hertz and Jane Mattes, "Donor-Shared Siblings or Genetic Strangers: New Families, Clans, and the Internet," *Journal of Family Issues* 32, no. 9 (September 2011): 1141, doi:10.1177/0192513X114043451135.

4. Daniels, Kramer, and Perez-y-Perez, "Semen Donors Who Are Open to Contact with Their Offspring: Issues and Implications for Them and Their Families," 670.

5. Alison Purdie, John C. Peek, Vivienne Adair, Freddie Graham, and Richard Fisher, "Ethics and Society: Attitudes of Parents of Young Children to Sperm Donation—Implications for Donor Recruitment," *Human Reproduction* 9, no. 7 (1994): 1355–58.

6. Matt Ridley, *Nature via Nurture: Genes, Experience, and What Makes Us Human* (New York: HarperCollins, 2003), 93.

Chapter 11

1. Roger Fisher and William Ury, *Getting to Yes: Negotiating Agreement without Giving In* (New York: Penguin Books, 1991), 56.

2. Daniel Goleman, "Email with Care," *Daniel Goleman: Emotional Intelligence, Social Intelligence, Ecological Intelligence*, October 8, 2007, http://danielgoleman .info/email-with-care.

Chapter 12

1. Charles A. Sims, Pamela Callum, Marilyn Ray, Jennifer Iger, and Rena E. Falk, "Genetic Testing of Sperm Donors: Survey of Current Practices," *Fertility and Sterility* 94, no. 1 (June 2010): 126–29.

2. Ken Daniels and Wendy Kramer, "Genetic and Health Issues Emerging from Sperm Donation: The Experiences and Views of Donors" (unpublished manuscript, 2013).

3. US Congress, Office of Technology Assessment, "Artificial Insemination: Practice in the United States: Summary of a 1987 Survey" (Washington, DC: US Government Printing Office, 1988), 3, http://www.princeton.edu/~ota/disk2/1988/8804/8804.PDF.

4. Blyth, Kramer, and Schneider, "Perspectives, Experiences, and Choices of Parents of Children Conceived Following Oocyte Donation," 179-188.

5. US Food and Drug Administration, Center for Biologics Evaluation and Research, "Guidance for Industry: Eligibility Determination for Donors of Human Cells, Tissues, and Cellular and Tissue-Based Products," 2007, http://www.fda.gov/BiologicsBloodVaccines/GuidanceCompliance RegulatoryInformation/Guidances/Tissue/ucm073964.htm.

6. Practice Committees of ASRM and SART. "Recommendations for Gamete and Embryo Donation: A Committee Opinion," *Fertility and Sterility* 99, no. 1 (2013): 47-62. http://download.journals.elsevierhealth.com/pdfs/journals/0015-0282/PIIS001502821202256X.pdf.

7. I. Glenn Cohen and Travis G. Coan, "Can You Buy Sperm Donor Identification?: An Experiment," *Journal of Empirical Legal Studies* 10, no. 4 (forthcoming December 2013).

index